Quotes
from Literature

Christopher Belton

Level 5

IBC パブリッシング

本書は、2014年に弊社から刊行された『世界文学の名言（Quotes from Literature）』の英文から項目をセレクトし、再編集したものです。

はじめに

　ラダーシリーズは、「はしご（ladder）」を使って一歩一歩上を目指すように、学習者の実力に合わせ、無理なくステップアップできるよう開発された英文リーダーのシリーズです。

　リーディング力をつけるためには、繰り返したくさん読むこと、いわゆる「多読」がもっとも効果的な学習法であると言われています。多読では、「1. 速く 2. 訳さず英語のまま 3. なるべく辞書を使わず」に読むことが大切です。スピードを計るなど、速く読むよう心がけましょう（たとえば TOEIC® テストの音声スピードはおよそ 1 分間に 150 語です）。そして 1 語ずつ訳すのではなく、英語を英語のまま理解するくせをつけるようにします。こうして読み続けるうちに語感がついてきて、だんだんと英語が理解できるようになるのです。まずは、ラダーシリーズの中からあなたのレベルに合った本を選び、少しずつ英文に慣れ親しんでください。たくさんの本を手にとるうちに、英文書がすらすら読めるようになってくるはずです。

《本シリーズの特徴》

- 中学校レベルから中級者レベルまで5段階に分かれています。自分に合ったレベルからスタートしてください。
- クラシックから現代文学、ノンフィクション、ビジネスと幅広いジャンルを扱っています。あなたの興味に合わせてタイトルを選べます。
- 巻末のワードリストで、いつでもどこでも単語の意味を確認できます。レベル1、2では、文中の全ての単語が、レベル3以上は中学校レベル外の単語が掲載されています。
- カバーにヘッドホーンマークのついているタイトルは、オーディオ・サポートがあります。ウェブから購入／ダウンロードし、リスニング教材としても併用できます。

《使用語彙について》

レベル1：中学校で学習する単語約1000語

レベル2：レベル1の単語＋使用頻度の高い単語約300語

レベル3：レベル1の単語＋使用頻度の高い単語約600語

レベル4：レベル1の単語＋使用頻度の高い単語約1000語

レベル5：語彙制限なし

Quotes
from
Literature

CONTENTS

読みはじめる前に

　本書ではチャールズ・ディケンズ、ウィリアム・シェイクスピア、ジェーン・オースティン、Ｌ・Ｍ・モンゴメリなどの名著から、現代人のこころに響くことばをテーマごとに集めました。古典文学から精選された宝石のような名文を、心ゆくまで味わいましょう。

名言の著者 ⇒で示されている作品は、本書に収録されている名言の原著名（邦訳）です。

Agatha Christie　アガサ・クリスティ（1890–1976）
　イギリス生まれの推理小説作家。世界的ベストセラーを記録し「ミステリーの女王」と呼ばれている。⇒『スタイルズ荘の怪事件』（p.9, 16）『秘密機関』（p.66, 83）

Aldous Huxley　オルダス・ハクスリー（1894–1963）
　イギリスの作家。20代で作家デビューし、風刺小説や評論を得意とした。後年は神秘主義や哲学の研究に関心を寄せた。⇒『クローム・イエロー』（p.54）

Algernon Blackwood　アルジャーノン・ブラックウッド（1869–1951）
　イギリスのホラー・ファンタジー作家。エディンバラ大学医学部中退。魔術結社「黄金の夜明け団」所属。⇒『木に愛された男』（p.10）『幻の下宿人』（p.37, 95）『柳』（p.77）『妖精郷の囚われ人』（p.27）

Anne Brontë　アン・ブロンテ（1820–1849）
　イギリス人作家。ブロンテ３姉妹の末妹で、３姉妹の中で最も宗教的で道徳的な作風であった。29歳で死去。⇒『アグネス・グレイ』（p.118）『ワイルドフェル・ホールの住人』（p.8, 64, 107）

Anthony Hope　アンソニー・ホープ（1863–1933）
　イギリス人作家、劇作家。冒険活劇の巨匠と称された。彼が作ったRuritanian という新しい形容詞は英語に加えられた。⇒『ドリーの会話』（p.122）

Anthony Trollope　アントニー・トロロープ（1815–1882）
　イギリス人作家。ヴィクトリア朝時代を代表する作家。郵便局員時代に郵便ポストを改良し普及させた人物でもある。⇒『バーチェスターの塔』（p.6, 103）『院長』（p.18）『ソーン医師』（p.21）

Arnold Bennett　アーノルド・ベネット（1867–1931）
　イギリスの小説家、劇作家、評論家。本格小説で評価を得る一方、大衆向け作品や、自己啓発書なども著した。⇒『称号』（p.21）

Benjamin Disraeli　ベンジャミン・ディズレーリ（1804–1881）
　イギリスの政治家、小説家。ユダヤ人。保守党党首となり、二期にわたって首相を務めた。⇒『ヴィヴィアン・グレイ』（p.30, 77）『若き公爵』（p.100）

『ヘンリエッタ・テンプル』(p.128)『アラコス伯爵の悲劇』(p.7, 10)『シビル』(p.23, 98, 99, 111)『カニングスビー』(p.43)『タンクレッド』(p.12)『ロゼアー』(p.5, 58)『エンディミオン』(p.90, 99)

Booth Tarkington　ブース・ターキントン（1869–1946）
アメリカの作家、劇作家。ピューリッツァー賞を2度受賞し、存命中に大成功を収めたベストセラー作家。⇒『偉大なるアンバーソン家の人々』(p.73)『アリス・アダムズ』(p.104)

Bram Stoker　ブラム・ストーカー（1847–1912）
イギリス、アイルランド生まれの小説家。怪奇小説の古典『吸血鬼ドラキュラ』の著者。演劇を好み、劇団の秘書業務や運営に携わった。⇒『吸血鬼ドラキュラ』(p.13, 30, 76, 115)

Charles Dickens　チャールズ・ディケンズ（1812–1870）
イギリスの作家。新聞記者を務めるかたわら著作を重ねデビュー。国民作家と評され紙幣に肖像が描かれるまでになった。⇒『ピクウィック・クラブ』(p.106)『オリバー・ツイスト』(p.5, 34, 40)『ニコラス・ニクルビー』(p.82)『骨董屋』(p.10, 64, 117)『バーナビー・ラッジ』(p.31, 51, 58, 61, 112, 125)『マーティン・チャズルウィット』(p.38)『ドンビー父子』(p.89)『デイヴィッド・コパーフィールド』(p.19, 32, 41, 45, 84, 98, 127)『荒涼館』(p.14, 19, 122)『リトル・ドリット』(p.15, 76)『大いなる遺産』(p.64)『憑かれた男』(p.45)『ハンフリー親方の時計』(p.8)『ゴールデン・メアリー号の難破』(p.124)

Charles Dudley Warner　チャールズ・ダドリー・ウォーナー（1829–1900）
アメリカの作家。編集者。マーク・トウェインの友人で、『金メッキ時代』の共著者。⇒『小さな旅』(p.91)『その運命』(p.119)

Charles Reade　チャールズ・リード（1814–1884）
イギリスの作家、劇作家。文学士号を取得後、研究員となり、古典文学博士号を取得。生涯を大学での研究に捧げた。⇒『クリスティ・ジョンストン』(p.6)

Charlotte Brontë　シャーロット・ブロンテ（1816–1855）
イギリスの作家。ブロンテ3姉妹の長姉。熱い情熱と反俗的精神が彼女の作風である。38歳で死去。⇒『ジェーン・エア』(p.4, 57)『ヴィレット』(p.8, 38, 80)

Daniel Defoe　ダニエル・デフォー（1660–1731）
イギリスの作家、ジャーナリスト。小説家として脚光を浴びるだけでなく、政治や宗教問題などについて論じた。⇒『ロビンソン・クルーソー』(p.3)『モル・フランダーズ』(p.32)

E. M. Forster　E・M・フォースター（1879–1970）
イギリスの作家。大学卒業後、世界各地を旅し体験をもとに執筆を行った。社会の壁を越えた人間の相互理解を描くのが特徴である。⇒『ハワーズ・エンド』(p.34, 67, 112)

Edgar Allan Poe エドガー・アラン・ポー（1809–1849）
アメリカの作家、雑誌編集者。放蕩な生活により大学を退学。常に困窮に
身を置きながら、ゴシック風の恐怖小説、推理小説を発表した。⇒『エレ
オノーラ』(p.116)

Edgar Rice Burroughs エドガー・ライス・バローズ（1875–1950）
アメリカの作家。『ターザン・シリーズ』をはじめとし数多くのSF作品を
著した。第二次世界大戦に従軍記者として参加、以後筆を折る。⇒『時間
に忘れられた国』(p.126, 128)

Edgar Wallace エドガー・ウォーレス（1875–1932）
イギリスの作家、ジャーナリスト。『キング・コング』の生みの親として
知られるが欧米ではミステリー作家として知られている。⇒『ねじれた蝋
燭の手がかり』(p.78)

Edith Wharton イーディス・ウォートン（1862–1937）
アメリカの上流階級に生まれ、11歳のころから著作を行う。女性として
最初のピューリッツァー賞受賞者。⇒『歓楽の家』(p.85, 86)

Elizabeth Gaskell エリザベス・ギャスケル（1810–1865）
イギリスの作家。9ヵ月の長男を亡くし、悲しみを癒すため筆を執る。人
間への共感と愛に満ちた作風が特徴。⇒『従妹フィリス』(p.15, 19)『妻た
ちと娘たち』(p.23, 32)

Elizabeth Stuart Phelps エリザベス・ステュアート・フェルプス
（1844–1911）
アメリカの作家、初期の女性解放運動家。後年は動物の権利を訴え、著作
にもその思想が反映されている。⇒『グェネヴィアの真実の物語』(p.106)

Emily Brontë エミリー・ブロンテ（1818–1848）
イギリスの作家。ブロンテ3姉妹の2番目。唯一の長編小説『嵐が丘』で
知られる。30歳で死去。⇒『嵐が丘』(p.38, 82, 129)

F. Scott Fitzgerald F・スコット・フィッツジェラルド（1896–1940）
アメリカの作家。失われた世代を代表する作家のひとり。社交界に身を
置き金銭トラブルに悩まされ続けた。⇒『華麗なるギャツビー』(p.79)『楽
園のこちら側』(p.116)

Florence L. Barclay フローレンス・L・バークリー（1862–1921）
イギリスのロマンス作家。牧師の家に生まれ、牧師と結婚し、8人の子供
の母となった。病床で著作を行った。⇒『ロザリオ』(p.20, 37, 52)

Frances Hodgson Burnett フランシス・ホジソン・バーネット（1849–1924）
イギリス出身。アメリカの作家、劇作家。児童書として書いた『小公子』
で一躍人気作家となった。⇒『秘密の花園』(p.49, 55, 63)

George Bernard Shaw ジョージ・バーナード・ショー（1856–1950）
イギリスで活躍したアイルランド出身の劇作家、評論家、社会主義者。
1952年にノーベル文学賞受賞。⇒『ピグマリオン』(p.104)『ウォレン夫人
の職業』(p.83)『人と超人』(p.107, 124)『恋をあさる人』(p.113)

George Eliot　ジョージ・エリオット（1819–1880）
　　イギリスの作家。本名はメアリー・アン・エヴァンズという女性。ヴィ
　　クトリア朝を代表する作家のひとり。⇒『アダム・ビード』（p.6, 30, 32, 84）
　　『フロス河の水車場』（p.23, 36, 45, 56, 62, 90, 120）『ミドルマーチ』（p.29,
　　38, 43, 86）

George Gissing　ジョージ・ギッシング（1857–1903）
　　イギリスの作家。労働者階級の悲惨さ、階級から疎外される苦しみなど
　　を描いた作品で知られる。⇒『三文文士』（p.60）『ヘンリー・ライクロフト
　　の私記』（p.129）

George Meredith　ジョージ・メレディス（1828–1909）
　　イギリスの作家。ウィットあふれる心理喜劇風の作品を多く残し、初期
　　の夏目漱石作品に影響を与えた。⇒『ハリー・リッチモンドの冒険』（p.13）
　　『サンドラ・ベローニ』（p.20）『十字路邸のダイアナ』（p.52, 93, 104）

Gilbert Parker　ギルバート・パーカー（1862–1932）
　　カナダ出身。イギリスの作家、政治家。帝国主義者。保守党員としてイギ
　　リス議会に籍を置いた。⇒『強者の戦い』（p.19, 81, 97）『フォルション夫人』
　　（p.43）『通行権』（p.84）『違反者』（p.96）『ある地方の寓話』（p.101, 111）

H. G. Wells　H・G・ウェルズ（1866–1946）
　　イギリスの作家、社会活動家、歴史家。SFの父と称されるひとり。⇒『宇
　　宙戦争』（p.78）『タイムマシン』（p.97, 98）

H. Rider Haggard　H・ライダー・ハガード（1856–1925）
　　イギリスの冒険、ファンタジー作家。秘境の地を舞台とした探検小説を
　　数多く残した。⇒『クレオパトラ』（p.59）『二人の女王』（p.94, 106）

Hans Christian Andersen　ハンス・クリスチャン・アンデルセン
（1805–1875）
　　デンマークの童話作家、詩人。彼の著作は世界中で愛読され、デンマーク
　　の旧紙幣には彼の肖像が描かれた。⇒『人魚姫』（p.125）

Harriet Beecher Stowe　ハリエット・ビーチャー・ストウ（1811–1896）
　　アメリカの作家、奴隷制度廃止論者。アメリカ初となる、黒人が主人公の
　　物語『アンクル・トムの小屋』を書き、奴隷制度に反対した。⇒『アンクル・
　　トムの小屋』（p.75, 79）

Henry Fielding　ヘンリー・フィールディング（1707–1754）
　　イギリスの劇作家、小説家。風刺劇で人気を博したが、政治批判のため法
　　律で上演を制限された。イギリス小説の父と呼ばれるひとり。⇒『トム・
　　ジョーンズ』（p.36）

Henry James　ヘンリー・ジェームズ（1843–1916）
　　アメリカ出身、イギリスで活躍した作家。アメリカ人と欧米人の両方の
　　視点を持ち、英米文学を代表する小説家として知られる。⇒『ある婦人の
　　肖像』（p.95）

Herman Melville　ハーマン・メルヴィル（1819–1891）
　　アメリカの作家。裕福な家庭に生まれるが、家が破産し経済的に困窮。職
　　を転々とし一時、捕鯨船の乗組員や水兵を務めた。⇒『白鯨』（p.77, 90）

J. Sheridan Le Fanu　J・シェリダン・レ・ファニュ（1814–1873）
　　アイルランドのホラー、ミステリー作家。ヴィクトリア朝期におけるアイ
　　ルランドホラーの父と目される。⇒『アンクル・サイラス』（p.28, 44）

James Joyce　ジェームズ・ジョイス（1882–1941）
　　アイルランド出身の作家、詩人。20世紀で最も偉大な作家のひとりに数
　　えられ、『ユリシーズ』は20世紀文学の最高傑作とも言われている。⇒『ユ
　　リシーズ』（p.5, 89）

James M. Barrie　ジェームズ・M・バリー（1860–1937）
　　スコットランド出身。イギリスの劇作家、ファンタジー作家。戯曲と
　　して書いた『ピーター・パン』で大成功を掴んだ。⇒『ピーター・パン』
　　（p.3, 55, 60）『小牧師』（p.27, 72）

Jane Austen　ジェーン・オースティン（1775–1817）
　　イギリスの作家。18世紀から19世紀イングランドにおける田舎の中流
　　社会に生き、その中に生きる女性を主に描いた。⇒『分別と多感』（p.94）『高
　　慢と偏見』（p.53, 60, 71, 82, 85, 102）『エマ』（p.86, 120）『説得』（p.113, 127）

Jerome K. Jerome　ジェローム・K・ジェローム（1859–1927）
　　イギリスの作家。ロンドンで困窮の中育ち、職を転々とし、最終的にユ
　　ーモア小説『ボートの三人男』で成功を手にした。⇒『ボートの三人男』
　　（p.64, 116）

John Galsworthy　ジョン・ゴールズワージー（1867–1933）
　　イギリスの作家。裕福な家庭に生まれ、オックスフォード大学に学ぶ。
　　家業の船舶業を手伝いながら世界を旅した。1932年ノーベル文学賞
　　を受賞。⇒『フォーサイト家の物語』（p.28, 50, 62, 102）『或る女の半生』
　　（p.117, 120）

John Webster　ジョン・ウェブスター（1580?–1634?）
　　イギリスの劇作家。エリザベス朝期、シェイクスピアと同時代に活躍し
　　た。作風は暗く陰鬱。⇒『白い悪魔』（p.33, 120）

Jonathan Swift　ジョナサン・スウィフト（1667–1745）
　　イングランド系アイルランド人。風刺作家、随筆家、詩人。司祭を務める
　　一方で、政治活動や文筆活動も行った。⇒『ガリヴァー旅行記』（p.81）

Joseph Conrad　ジョゼフ・コンラッド（1857–1924）
　　ポーランド出身。イギリスの作家。商船の船員を務め世界各地を航海し
　　た。海洋文学で知られる。⇒『西欧人の眼に』（p.8, 32）

Jules Verne　ジュール・ヴェルヌ（1828–1905）
　　フランスの作家。科学、冒険小説を数多く残し、SFの父と呼ばれるひと
　　り。⇒『地底旅行』（p.30）『海底二万マイル』（p.39）

Kate Chopin ケイト・ショパン（1851–1904）
　アメリカの作家。裕福な家に生まれ、夫との死別後、執筆を始める。女性の性的な開放を描いた『目覚め』は評価を得るまでに半世紀以上を要した。⇒『目覚め』(p.126)

L. Frank Baum L・フランク・ボーム（1856–1919）
　アメリカのファンタジー、児童文学作家。戯曲家、俳優としても活動した。⇒『オズの魔法使い』(p.11, 100)

Louisa May Alcott ルイザ・メイ・オールコット（1832–1888）
　アメリカの作家。家計のため様々な職に就き、生涯独身であった。自らの体験と家庭環境を元に書いた『若草物語』で一躍流行作家となった。⇒『若草物語』(p.34, 108)『第三若草物語』(p.90, 102)

Lucy Maud Montgomery ルーシー・モード・モンゴメリ（1874–1942）
　カナダの作家。教師を務めた後、祖母の世話をしながら執筆した『赤毛のアン』シリーズが世界的ベストセラーとなった。⇒『赤毛のアン』(p.76)『アンの青春』(p.8, 18, 50, 51, 58, 66, 93, 101)『アンの愛情』(p.43, 96)『アンの夢の家』(p.120)

Mark Twain マーク・トウェイン（1835–1910）
　アメリカの作家。アメリカ文学の父と目される。数多くの小説やエッセーを発表し、世界中で講演活動を行う当世の著名人であった。⇒『アーサー王宮廷のコネチカット・ヤンキー』(p.12, 96, 115)『王子と乞食』(p.54)『まぬけのウィルソン』(p.72)

Mary Shelley メアリ・シェリー（1797–1851）
　イギリスの作家。ゴシック小説『フランケンシュタイン』で知られ、SFの先駆者、あるいは創始者と呼ばれている。⇒『フランケンシュタイン』(p.34, 56)

Myrtle Reed マートル・リード（1874–1911）
　アメリカの作家、詩人、ジャーナリスト、および慈善活動家。オリーブ・グリーンの別名で料理本も多く出版した。⇒『オールドローズと銀』(p.22)

O. Henry O・ヘンリー（1862–1910）
　アメリカの作家。掌編、短編小説の名手として知られる。横領の容疑で有罪判決を受け、服役中ひそかに小説を投稿し出版していた。⇒『真面目な話』(p.6)

Oliver Goldsmith オリヴァー・ゴールドスミス（1730–1774）
　アイルランド出身。イギリスの作家、劇作家、詩人。大学卒業後、文筆活動で生計を立てるが生涯貧しかった。⇒『ウェイクフィールドの牧師』(p.74, 121)

Oliver Wendell Holmes, Sr. オリヴァー・ウェンデル・ホームズ（1809–1894）
　アメリカの作家、医学者。優れた作家としてだけではなく、医学の改革者としても名を残した。⇒『朝食テーブルの独裁者』(p.59, 100)『朝食テーブルの教授』(p.128)『エルシー・ヴェナー』(p.126)

Oscar Wilde　オスカー・ワイルド（1854–1900）
アイルランド出身の作家、劇作家、詩人。耽美主義、退廃芸術の旗手と目される。多彩な文筆活動と奇抜な言動で耳目を集めた。⇒『ドリアン・グレイの肖像』(p.42, 52, 67, 92)『アーサー・サヴィル卿の犯罪』(p.105)『ウィンダミア卿夫人の扇』(p.7, 41, 123)『つまらぬ女』(p.17, 91)

Owen Wister　オーウェン・ウィスター（1860–1938）
アメリカの作家。ハーバード大学、ハーバード法科大学卒業。セオドア・ルーズベルト大統領のクラスメイトであった。西部劇の父と称される。⇒『ヴァージニアン』(p.31)

P. G. Wodehouse　P・G・ウッドハウス（1881–1975）
イギリスの作家。20世紀最大とも称されるユーモア作家。銀行員の副業として執筆していたが、人気を博し専業作家となった。⇒『上の階の男』(p.92)

Rudyard Kipling　ラドヤード・キップリング（1865–1936）
イギリスの作家、詩人。イギリス統治下のインドを舞台にした作品で知られる。史上最年少、イギリス人初のノーベル文学賞受賞者。⇒『勇敢な船長たち』(p.71)

Samuel Butler　サミュエル・バトラー（1835–1902）
イギリスの作家。因習が揺らぎ始めるヴィクトリア朝後期に生き、キリスト教の正当性の研究、進化論の研究など多彩な業績で知られる。⇒『万人の道』(p.17, 49, 58, 67)

Sir Arthur Conan Doyle　アーサー・コナン・ドイル（1859–1930）
スコットランド出身。イギリスの作家、医師。推理小説の生みの親として知られるが、歴史小説、SF作品も多く残した。⇒『花婿失踪事件』(p.124)『オレンジの種五つ』(p.29)『唇のねじれた男』(p.22)『独身の貴族』(p.35, 61)『ぶな屋敷』(p.56)『最後の事件』(p.4)『失われた世界』(p.122)『毒ガス帯』(p.73)『白衣の騎士団』(p.15)『茶色い手』(p.78)『革の漏斗』(p.100)『呪われた前夜』(p.74, 80)『都市郊外で』(p.15)『我が家のダービー競馬』(p.106)『スターク・マンローからの手紙』(p.28, 41)

Sir Max Beerbohm　マックス・ビアボーム（1872–1956）
イギリスの作家、批評家、風刺画家。機知あふれる短編の名手として知られるが、唯一の長編小説『ズリイカ・ドブソン』も好評を博した。⇒『ズリイカ・ドブソン』(p.36)

Stephen Crane　スティーヴン・クレイン（1871–1900）
アメリカの作家、詩人。アメリカ自然主義文学の先駆者として後代の作家に影響を与えた。28歳の若さで亡くなった。⇒『赤い武功章』(p.11)

Theodore Dreiser　セオドア・ドライサー（1871–1945）
アメリカの作家。貧しい移民の家に生まれ、様々な職を経て新聞記者を務めた。死後に評価を受け、現在ではアメリカ文学の父と称されている。⇒『シスター・キャリー』(p.16)

Thomas Hardy　トマス・ハーディ（1840–1928）
　　イギリスの作家、詩人、建築家。現在では自然主義の古典として世界中で
　　愛読されている小説が生前は評価を受けず、詩を多く残した。⇒『はるか
　　群衆を離れて』(p.19, 21)『エセルバータの手』(p.105)

Virginia Woolf　ヴァージニア・ウルフ（1882–1941）
　　イギリスの作家、評論家。モダニズム文学の旗手といわれ、20世紀イギリ
　　ス文学を代表する作家のひとり。⇒『ジェイコブの部屋』(p.54)

W. Somerset Maugham　W・サマセット・モーム（1874–1965）
　　イギリスの作家、劇作家、医師。成功した文筆業の一方で、軍医、諜報部
　　員、情報工作員として活躍した。⇒『月と六ペンス』(p.114)

Wilkie Collins　ウィルキー・コリンズ（1824–1889）
　　イギリスの作家、劇作家。ヴィクトリア朝の人気作家であり、初期の推理
　　小説作家。『白衣の女』は伝説的な大ヒットとなり一躍時の人となった。
　　⇒『白衣の女』(p.31, 123)『月長石』(p.40, 67, 121)『アーマデイル』(p.53)

Willa Cather　ウィラ・キャザー（1873–1947）
　　アメリカの作家。高校教師、雑誌編集者を勤めながら創作に励み、1923
　　年にピューリッツァー賞を受賞した。⇒『マイ・アントニーア』(p.21)『わ
　　れらの仲間』(p.64)『おお開拓者たちよ！』(p.118)

William Congreve　ウィリアム・コングリーヴ（1670–1729）
　　イギリスの劇作家。処女作の喜劇『老独身者』が絶賛を浴び、続く喜劇の
　　数々も好評を博した。唯一の悲劇『喪服の花嫁』で名声を不動のものとし
　　た。⇒『老独身者』(p.43)

William Makepeace Thackeray　ウィリアム・メイクピース・サッカレー
（1811–1863）
　　インド生まれのイギリス人作家。上流階級を痛烈に批判した『虚栄の市』
　　で文名を高め、ヴィクトリア朝を代表する作家のひとりとなった。⇒『虚
　　栄の市』(p.14, 56, 62, 75, 114, 119)『ヘンリー・エズモンド』(p.13, 41)

William Shakespeare　ウィリアム・シェイクスピア（1564–1616）
　　イギリスの劇作家、詩人。イギリス・ルネサンス演劇を代表する人物。
　　最も優れた英文学の作家と称されている。⇒『ロミオとジュリエット』
　　(p.65, 74, 102)『ジュリアス・シーザー』(p.4)『ハムレット』(p.44, 80, 115)
　　『リア王』(p.15)『コリオレイナス』(p.50)『間違いの喜劇』(p.35)『じゃじゃ
　　馬ならし』(p.71)『ヴェニスの商人』(p.92)『お気に召すまま』(p.82)『終わり
　　よければすべてよし』(p.33)『ヘンリー六世　第一部』(p.103)『リチャード
　　二世』(p.33)『ヴィーナスとアドニス』(p.4)

Chapter 1

Things that Make us Stronger

Chapter 1
【力づけてくれるもの】

小説の世界を通して、わたしたち読者は危険を冒すような旅や、現実とは異なるさまざまな人との出会いを経験します。登場人物たちが起こす行動や、彼らが語る示唆に富んだ言葉は、ときにわたしたちを励まし、勇気を与えてくれるでしょう。こうした読書経験を積み重ねながら、現実の世界でも一歩ずつ前に進んでいきたいですね。

Vocabulary わからない語は巻末のワードリストで確認しましょう。

- [ ] valiant
- [ ] acquirement
- [ ] conscience
- [ ] dare
- [ ] puberty
- [ ] devoted
- [ ] subtle
- [ ] earnest
- [ ] matrimony
- [ ] frankness

Pick Up 名言の一部を和訳と共に読んで、含蓄を味わいましょう。

An appreciative listener is always stimulating. (よい聞き手はいつも励ましを与えてくれる) (⇒ p.9)

We are all drifting reefwards now, and faith is our only anchor. (今やわれわれはみな暗礁に向かって漂流している。信仰だけが唯一の錨だ) (⇒ p.13)

More helpful than all wisdom is one draught of simple human pity that will not forsake us. (知恵の限りを尽くしてもらうことより助けとなるのは、私たちを見捨てることのない単純で人間らしい憐れみを、ただ一度でもかけてもらうことだ) (⇒ p.23)

Adventure

Everybody loves adventure. But the word is also often synonymous with "danger," which is why so many of the quotes listed here include a "danger" connotation. Few people enjoy being in danger. However, it is a different story in a novel. The dangers you experience in fiction can be thrilling. One of my favorite quotes is from Daniel Defoe's *Robinson Crusoe* listed below. How often do we flinch at the dangers we envision in our minds and fail to take the action we need to take?

"To die will be an awfully big adventure."

—James M. Barrie, *Peter Pan*

Fear of danger is ten thousand times more terrifying than danger itself.

—Daniel Defoe, *Robinson Crusoe*

"I think that you know me well enough, Watson, to understand that I am by no means a nervous man. At the same time, it is stupidity rather than courage to refuse to recognize danger when it is close upon you."

—Sir Arthur Conan Doyle, *The Final Problem*

It is in vain to say human beings ought to be satisfied with tranquillity: they must have action; and they will make it if they cannot find it.

—Charlotte Brontë, *Jane Eyre*

"The path is smooth that leadeth on to danger."

—William Shakespeare, *Venus and Adonis*

"Cowards die many times before their deaths; the valiant never taste of death but once."

—William Shakespeare, *Julius Caesar*

Art and Literature

Writers have competed to come up with words that strike at the heart of this all-encompassing theme of art and literature. Some have been witty, some have been thought-provoking, but the common denominator among artists has been their dislike of critics. This can be seen in the following words of Benjamin Disraeli. Another famous quote that dealt a blow to the critics is composer Jean Sibelius' "No statue has ever been put up to a critic."

The supreme question about a work of art is out of how deep a life does it spring.

——James Joyce, *Ulysses*

"There are books of which the backs and covers are by far the best parts."

——Charles Dickens, *Oliver Twist*

"You know who the critics are? The men who have failed in literature and art."

——Benjamin Disraeli, *Lothair*

"Art is not imitation, but illusion."
——Charles Reade, *Christie Johnstone*

There is no royal road to learning; no short cut to the acquirement of any art.
——Anthony Trollope, *Barchester Towers*

A story with a moral appended is like the bill of a mosquito. It bores you, and then injects a stinging drop to irritate your conscience.
——O. Henry, *Strictly Business*

How is it that the poets have said so many fine things about our first love, so few about our later love? Are their first poems their best?
——George Eliot, *Adam Bede*

Communication

The meaning of the word "communication" is changing with the advancement of technology. These days, this word probably brings to mind e-mail, cellphone mail, and the Internet. Literature reminds us that communication is not a matter between a man and a machine, but between two or more people. Incidentally, the following words of Oscar Wilde have a deeper meaning than they appear: "talking to a brick wall" is an idiom that means that whatever you say is ignored by the other person. For example, "Talking to my wife is like talking to a brick wall."

The fool wonders, the wise man asks.

—Benjamin Disraeli, *Count Alarcos: A Tragedy*

"I like talking to a brick wall—it's the only thing in the world that never contradicts me!"

—Oscar Wilde, *Lady Windermere's Fan*

"If we can only speak to slander our betters, let us hold our tongues."

—Anne Brontë, *The Tenant of Wildfell Hall*

❦

Silence is of different kinds, and breathes different meanings.

—Charlotte Brontë, *Villette*

❦

To conceal anything from those to whom I am attached, is not in my nature. I can never close my lips where I have opened my heart.

—Charles Dickens, *Master Humphrey's Clock*

❦

Words, as is well known, are the great foes of reality.

—Joseph Conrad, *Under Western Eyes*

❦

"When you've learned to laugh at the things that should be laughed at, and not to laugh at those that shouldn't, you've got wisdom and understanding."

—Lucy Maud Montgomery, *Anne of the Island*

An appreciative listener is always stimulating.
—Agatha Christie, *The Mysterious Affair at Styles*

Courage

Acts of courage are highly praised, so much so that it is considered that a man is not a man unless he is courageous. However, if we look at how courage is portrayed in literature, any man may have the courage to display it when the occasion calls for it. On the other hand, in the words of Benjamin Disraeli, a lack of courage often leads onto bullying, which is considered the most despicable act of all.

Courage is fire, and bullying is smoke.

——Benjamin Disraeli, *Count Alarcos: A Tragedy*

Resignation brings a curious large courage—when there is nothing more to lose. The soul takes risks, and dares.

——Algernon Blackwood, *The Man Whom the Trees Loved*

The Sun himself is weak when he first rises, and gathers strength and courage as the day gets on.

——Charles Dickens, *The Old Curiosity Shop*

"You have plenty of courage, I am sure," answered Oz. "All you need is confidence in yourself. There is no living thing that is not afraid when it faces danger. The true courage is in facing danger when you are afraid, and that kind of courage you have in plenty."

——L. Frank Baum, *The Wonderful Wizard of Oz*

At times he regarded the wounded soldiers in an envious way. He conceived persons with torn bodies to be peculiarly happy. He wished that he, too, had a wound, a red badge of courage.

——Stephen Crane, *The Red Badge of Courage*

Faith

The word faith is used in a variety of contexts, such as an unshakable faith in God through to a frivolous faith in winning the lottery. While many writers believe that nothing can be accomplished without faith (or belief), there are others who have taken the opposite position, believing that faith is overrated and should not be a top priority in everyday life. For example, Voltaire said, "Faith consists in believing when it is beyond the power of reason to believe," and Friedrich Nietzsche said "Faith: not wanting to know what is true." I personally believe in the former.

"I hold that duty cannot exist without faith."

—Benjamin Disraeli, *Tancred*

Any mummery will cure if the patient's faith is strong in it.

—Mark Twain, *A Connecticut Yankee in King Arthur's Court*

"'Tis not the dying for a faith that's so hard, Master

Harry—every man of every nation has done that—'tis the living up to it that is difficult."

—William Makepeace Thackeray,
The History of Henry Esmond

"Faith works miracles. At least it allows time for them."

——George Meredith, *The Adventures of Harry Richmond*

We are all drifting reefwards now, and faith is our only anchor.

——Bram Stoker, *Dracula*

Family

People perceive the family in different ways, but the general view of literature is that it is a blessing up until puberty, a burden during the teens, and an embarrassment after reaching adulthood. But, conversely, children can also be a blessing, a burden or an embarrassment at any stage of their lives. As Michael Levine said, "Having children makes you no more a parent than having a piano makes you a pianist."

It is a melancholy truth that even great men have their poor relations.

——Charles Dickens, *Bleak House*

If a man has committed wrong in life, I don't know any moralist more anxious to point his errors out to the world than his own relations.

——William Makepeace Thackeray, *Vanity Fair*

Her look at her father, half admiring him and proud of him, half ashamed for him, all devoted and loving, went to his inmost heart.

——Charles Dickens, *Little Dorrit*

※

"There is many a young cockerel that will stand upon a dunghill and crow about his father, by way of making his own plumage to shine."

——Elizabeth Gaskell, *Cousin Phillis*

※

"How sharper than a serpent's tooth it is to have a thankless child!"

——William Shakespeare, *King Lear*

※

"Streams may spring from one source, and yet some be clear and some be foul."

——Sir Arthur Conan Doyle, *The White Company*

※

To see their sons and daughters so flushed and healthy and happy, gave them also a reflected glow, and it was hard to say who had most pleasure from the game, those who played or those who watched.

——Sir Arthur Conan Doyle, *Beyond the City*

Instinct

Instinct, by its very nature, is difficult to understand and describe. Birds know by instinct that they must fly south for the winter, and small creatures know by instinct the animals that will prey on them. Instinct protects us. It encourages us to fear heights from which a fall would be fatal, it closes our eyes when hot oil spat from a frying pan is heading toward us, and it teaches us to loathe the creatures that nature has equipped with poison. It is also thought to point us in the direction of the one true love that would be our soul mate, although, unfortunately, very few people are able to attest to this.

"Instinct is a marvellous thing," mused Poirot. "It can neither be explained nor ignored."

——Agatha Christie, *The Mysterious Affair at Styles*

Our civilization is still in a middle stage, scarcely beast in that it is no longer wholly guided by instinct; scarcely human, in that it is not yet wholly guided by reason.

——Theodore Dreiser, *Sister Carrie*

"Men always want to be a woman's first love. That is their clumsy vanity. We women have a more subtle instinct about things. What we like is to be a man's last romance."

— Oscar Wilde, *A Woman of No Importance*

Young as he was, his instinct told him that the best liar is he who makes the smallest amount of lying go the longest way.

— Samuel Butler, *The Way of All Flesh*

Language

The title of this section may, perhaps, be misleading, since the first thing that comes to mind when we hear the word "language" is the languages used by the countries around the world to define their cultures. In this case, however, the predominant way in which language is treated in literature has nothing to do with each independent language, but tends to concentrate on the way in which language is used. Needless to say, the language referred to in the quotations listed below is the English language.

We are never half so interesting when we have learned that language is given us to enable us to conceal our thoughts.

——Lucy Maud Montgomery, *Anne of the Island*

"A spoken word, Sir Abraham, is often of more value than volumes of written advice."

——Anthony Trollope, *The Warden*

I am . . . joined with eleven others in reporting the

debates in Parliament for a Morning Newspaper. Night after night, I record predictions that never come to pass, professions that are never fulfilled, explanations that are only meant to mystify. I wallow in words.

——Charles Dickens, *David Copperfield*

※

"It is difficult for a woman to define her feelings in language which is chiefly made by men to express theirs."

——Thomas Hardy, *Far From The Madding Crowd*

※

"A word in earnest is as good as a speech."

——Charles Dickens, *Bleak House*

※

"Really it is very wholesome exercise, this trying to make one's words represent one's thoughts, instead of merely looking to their effect on others."

——Elizabeth Gaskell, *Cousin Phillis*

※

He knew the lie of silence to be as evil as the lie of speech.

——Gilbert Parker, *The Battle of the Strong*

Marriage

Marriage often comes in for a lot of ridicule in literature. Characters in books are accused of having ulterior motives for getting married, and marriage itself tends to be depicted as a period of boredom that follows the fun of courtship. One of the most famous sayings about marriage is, "Marry in haste, repent at leisure." This saying has been around since the end of the 17th century, when it was first expressed in print in William Congreve's *The Old Batchelour*, and it has since turned into a well-known proverb. This, of course, is true. Marriage requires dedication and commitment, and the decision to marry must be considered deeply before taking the plunge.

"Marriage is not a mere question of sentiment. It has to wear. It has to last. It must have a solid and dependable foundation, to stand the test and strain of daily life together."

——Florence L. Barclay, *The Rosary*

"A marriage without love is dishonour."

——George Meredith, *Sandra Belloni*

🏃

"Being a husband is a whole-time job. That's why so many husbands fail. They can't give their entire attention to it."

——Arnold Bennett, *The Title*

🏃

It appears that ordinary men take wives because possession is not possible without marriage, and that ordinary women accept husbands because marriage is not possible without possession.

——Thomas Hardy, *Far From The Madding Crowd*

🏃

"Men are all right for friends, but as soon as you marry them they turn into cranky old fathers, even the wild ones. They begin to tell you what's sensible and what's foolish, and want you to stick at home all the time. I prefer to be foolish when I feel like it, and be accountable to nobody."

——Willa Cather, *My Antonia*

🏃

There is no road to wealth so easy and respectable as that of matrimony.

——Anthony Trollope, *Doctor Thorne*

Wisdom

Unlike intelligence, wisdom is gained through experience. Hence, the more experience one gains, the wiser one becomes. Oh, I wish this were true. Some people, whatever they gain from their experiences, lead completely fruitless lives. The British writer J. L. Carr summed up such people beautifully in *The Harpole Report*: "You have not had thirty years' experience... You have had one year's experience thirty times." I have met several people who fit this description perfectly.

"I confess that I have been as blind as a mole, but it is better to learn wisdom late than never to learn it at all."

——Sir Arthur Conan Doyle, *The Man with the Twisted Lip*

"Silence and reserve will give anyone a reputation for wisdom."

——Myrtle Reed, *Old Rose and Silver*

"But sometimes one likes foolish people for their

folly, better than wise people for their wisdom."

——Elizabeth Gaskell, *Wives and Daughters*

꙯

"There is no wisdom like frankness."

——Benjamin Disraeli, *Sybil*

꙯

More helpful than all wisdom is one draught of simple human pity that will not forsake us.

——George Eliot, *The Mill on the Floss*

Chapter 2

Things that
Lead to Sadness

Chapter 2
【悲しみに導くもの】

わたしたちは年齢を重ねていくうえで、大なり小なり、悲しみを避けて通ることはできません。文学においては、それが自分の過ちによって生まれるものか、はたまた手に負えない運命の仕業として描かれています。作家たちは、しかし、言葉を尽くして、また生きてさえいれば希望が訪れることも教えてくれるのです。

Vocabulary わからない語は巻末のワードリストで確認しましょう。

- ☐ humility
- ☐ malleable
- ☐ intriguing
- ☐ covetousness
- ☐ poignant
- ☐ lamentation
- ☐ venom
- ☐ sting
- ☐ repent
- ☐ smarting

Pick Up 名言の一部を和訳と共に読んで、含蓄を味わいましょう。

But what we call our despair is often only the painful eagerness of unfed hope. (絶望と呼ばれているものの多くは、かなえられない希望を痛ましくも必死に追い求めることにすぎない)（⇒ p.29）

What loneliness is more lonely than distrust? (他人を信じられないこと以上にわびしい孤独などあるだろうか)（⇒ p.38）

"We should regret our mistakes and learn from them, but never carry them forward into the future with us." (私たちは自分の過ちから学ぶべきですが、過ちを将来にまで持ち越してはいけません)（⇒ p.43）

Aging

Getting older has a very bad reputation. Young people think that old age is something that will never happen to them, and old people simply believe that they are getting closer and closer to the grave. It is true that as we age, our health suffers and our strength declines, but we also tend to become stubborn, prejudiced, superior, and forgetful. Aging, however, is not without its good points. It teaches us patience, common sense, wisdom, humility and compassion. Literature approaches age from both sides of the spectrum, as can be seen below.

"When you are older you will know that life is a long lesson in humility."

——James M. Barrie, *The Little Minister*

"At forty you stand upon the threshold of life, with values learned and rubbish cleared away."

——Algernon Blackwood, *A Prisoner in Fairyland*

There comes with old age a time when the heart is no longer fusible or malleable, and must retain the form in which it has cooled down.

——J. Sheridan Le Fanu, *Uncle Silas*

James had passed through the fire, but he had passed also through the river of years which washes out the fire; he had experienced the saddest experience of all-forgetfulness of what it was like to be in love.

——John Galsworthy, *The Forsyte Saga*

At last, however, his conversation became unbearable—a foul young man is odious, but a foul old one is surely the most sickening thing on earth.

——Sir Arthur Conan Doyle, *The Stark Munro Letters*

Despair

Despair is sometimes confused with disappointment. People claim that they despair of ever finding a suitable partner, of finishing an item of work in time, or of passing an examination. This is not despair; only the people who have truly experienced it will recognize it. Norwegian writer Jo Nesbo summed up despair as follows: "Losing your life is not the worst thing that can happen. The worst thing is to lose your reason for living."

"Tut! tut!" cried Sherlock Holmes. "You must act, man, or you are lost. Nothing but energy can save you. This is no time for despair."

———Sir Arthur Conan Doyle, *The Five Orange Pips*

But what we call our despair is often only the painful eagerness of unfed hope.

———George Eliot, *Middlemarch*

For there is no despair so absolute as that which comes with the first moments of our first great sorrow, when we have not yet known what it is to have suffered and be healed, to have despaired and to have recovered hope.

——George Eliot, *Adam Bede*

The Disappointment of Manhood succeeds to the delusion of Youth: let us hope that the heritage of Old Age is not Despair.

——Benjamin Disraeli, *Vivian Grey*

Despair has its own calms.

——Bram Stoker, *Dracula*

"As long as the heart beats, as long as body and soul keep together, I cannot admit that any creature endowed with a will has need to despair of life."

——Jules Verne, *Journey to the Center of the Earth*

Evil

Literature deals extensively with the concept of evil, and many books base their entire plotlines on the battle between good and evil. From this point of view, we come into more contact with evil in books than we do in any other medium in our daily lives. The reason why this excites us is probably because the concept of people becoming evil is an intriguing subject. However, evil is only interesting in books because we know that it will not prevail. Good will always win over.

"But recollect from this time that all good things perverted to evil purposes, are worse than those which are naturally bad."

——Charles Dickens, *Barnaby Rudge*

"There are worse evils than war."

——Owen Wister, *The Virginian*

The best men are not consistent in good—why should the worst men be consistent in evil?

——Wilkie Collins, *The Woman in White*

❦

As covetousness is the root of all evil, so poverty is, I believe, the worst of all snares.

——Daniel Defoe, *Moll Flanders*

❦

"I hope that real love and truth are stronger in the end than any evil or misfortune in the world."

——Charles Dickens, *David Copperfield*

❦

"A belief in a supernatural source of evil is not necessary; men alone are quite capable of every wickedness."

——Joseph Conrad, *Under Western Eyes*

❦

"How easy it is to judge rightly after one sees what evil comes from judging wrongly."

——Elizabeth Gaskell, *Wives and Daughters*

❦

"Men's lives are as thoroughly blended with each other as the air they breathe: evil spreads as necessarily as disease."

——George Eliot, *Adam Bede*

Grief

Grief is almost impossible to describe, but it is something that we must all experience at least several times in our lives. Grief is also immeasurable. It is impossible to say if the loss of a beloved pet causes more grief than love lost. Authors have striven since time immemorial to put the essence of grief into words: some more successfully than others. One of the most poignant quotations probably exists on a gravestone in Ireland, as follows: "Death leaves a heartache no one can heal, love leaves a memory no one can steal."

"Grief makes one hour ten."

——William Shakespeare, *King Richard II*

We think cag'd birds sing, when indeed they cry.

——John Webster, *The White Devil*

"Moderate lamentation is the right of the dead: excessive grief the enemy to the living."

——William Shakespeare, *All's Well That Ends Well*

❧

The agony of my feelings allowed me no respite; no incident occurred from which my rage and misery could not extract its food.

——Mary Shelley, *Frankenstein*

❧

Joy and grief were mingled in the cup; but there were no bitter tears: for even grief itself arose so softened, and clothed in such sweet and tender recollections, that it became a solemn pleasure, and lost all character of pain.

——Charles Dickens, *Oliver Twist*

❧

The crime of suicide lies rather in its disregard for the feelings of those whom we leave behind.

——E. M. Forster, *Howards End*

❧

"I never wanted to go away, and the hard part now is the leaving you all. I'm not afraid, but it seems as if I should be homesick for you even in heaven."

——Louisa May Alcott, *Little Women*

Jealousy

William Shakespeare's mention of the "green-eyed monster" in *Othello* represents the first time that jealousy was attributed with a color. It was from this that the common English phrase "green with envy" was coined. Jealousy is the bane of mankind, and it is a central motif in a large number of novels. Jealousy breeds hatred, which provides the motive for murder. Jealousy leads to greed, which provides the motive for theft. Jealousy leads to desire, which provides the motive for adultery. From this point of view, it may be assumed that authors are in favor of jealousy. After all, books about jealousy sell well.

"Jealousy is a strange transformer of characters."
—Sir Arthur Conan Doyle,
The Adventure of the Noble Bachelor

"The venom clamours of a jealous woman Poisons more deadly than a mad dog's tooth."
—William Shakespeare, *The Comedy of Errors*

When the effects of female jealousy do not appear openly in their proper colours of rage and fury, we may suspect that mischievous passion to be at work privately, and attempting to undermine, what it doth not attack above-ground.

——Henry Fielding, *Tom Jones*

Jealousy is never satisfied with anything short of an omniscience that would detect the subtlest fold of the heart.

——George Eliot, *The Mill on the Floss*

But the dullard's envy of brilliant men is always assuaged by the suspicion that they will come to a bad end.

——Sir Max Beerbohm, *Zuleika Dobson*

Anger and jealousy can no more bear to lose sight of their objects than love.

——George Eliot, *The Mill on the Floss*

Loneliness

It is said that everything must be taken in moderation, and this is especially true for loneliness. A little bit of solitude is something we all like. It provides us with the time to relax while we read, listen to music, stare contentedly at the beauty of nature, or contemplate our own thoughts. Too much loneliness, however, can be a form of torture once the heart begins to crave companionship. The strange thing about loneliness is that we want it went we don't have it, and don't want it when we have it.

I wish I were not quite so lonely—and so poor. And yet I love both my loneliness and my poverty. The former makes me appreciate the companionship of the wind and rain, while the latter preserves my liver and prevents me wasting time in dancing attendance upon women.

—Algernon Blackwood, *The Listener*

"The liberty to live for self alone becomes in time a weary bondage."

—Florence L. Barclay, *The Rosary*

❦

Peril, loneliness, an uncertain future, are not oppressive evils, so long as the frame is healthy and the faculties are employed; so long, especially, as Liberty lends us her wings, and Hope guides us by her star.

——Charlotte Brontë, *Villette*

❦

It was one of those hot, silent nights, when people sit at windows listening for the thunder which they know will shortly break; when they recall dismal tales of hurricanes and earthquakes; and of lonely travellers on open plains, and lonely ships at sea, struck by lightning.

——Charles Dickens, *Martin Chuzzlewit*

❦

What loneliness is more lonely than distrust?

——George Eliot, *Middlemarch*

❦

"I am now quite cured of seeking pleasure in society, be it country or town. A sensible man ought to find sufficient company in himself."

——Emily Brontë, *Wuthering Heights*

"The sea is everything. It covers seven tenths of the terrestrial globe. Its breath is pure and healthy. It is an immense desert, where man is never lonely, for he feels life stirring on all sides."

——Jules Verne, *20,000 Leagues Under the Sea*

Misfortune

Misfortune visits everyone at regular intervals. At least, so we tell ourselves. But, maybe what we put down to bad luck is, in fact, more likely to be our own carelessness. We blame misfortune for losing our keys, when it is us who mislaid them. We blame misfortune for denting the car fender, when it is us who hit the wall. We blame misfortune for the supermarket selling out of bread, when it is us who arrived too late. Real misfortune is the work of fate, and whatever the result, it is beyond the control of mere humans.

"This is a miserable world," says the Sergeant. "Human life, Mr. Betteredge, is a sort of target—misfortune is always firing at it, and always hitting the mark."

——Wilkie Collins, *The Moonstone*

Surprises, like misfortunes, seldom come alone.

——Charles Dickens, *Oliver Twist*

"We must meet reverses boldly, and not suffer

them to frighten us, my dear. We must learn to act the play out. We must live misfortune down, Trot!"

——Charles Dickens, *David Copperfield*

"Misfortunes one can endure—they come from outside, they are accidents. But to suffer for one's own faults—ah!—there is the sting of life."

——Oscar Wilde, *Lady Windermere's Fan*

'Tis misfortune that awakens ingenuity, or fortitude, or endurance, in hearts where these qualities had never come to life but for the circumstance which gave them a being.

——William Makepeace Thackeray, *The History of Henry Esmond*

Are you conscious of the restful influence which the stars exert? To me they are the most soothing things in Nature. I am proud to say that I don't know the name of one of them. The glamour and romance would pass away from them if they were all classified and ticketed in one's brain. But when a man is hot and flurried, and full of his own little ruffled dignities and infinitesimal misfortunes, then a star bath is the finest thing in the world.

——Sir Arthur Conan Doyle, *The Stark Munro Letters*

Regret

We all have regrets, but as the past cannot be rewritten, we have no choice but to learn to live with them. But, it is our regrets as much as our satisfactions that shape the person we are. The ability to feel regret is a form of compassion, in that it confirms the fact that we have the moral fiber to repent over past actions. From this point of view, the more regrets we have, the more compassionate we are. However, it is also possible to feel regret over an action not taken. American journalist and humorist Helen Rowland summed this up perfectly when she said, "The follies which a man regrets most in his life are those which he didn't commit when he had the opportunity."

"Nowadays most people die of a sort of creeping common sense, and discover when it is too late that the only things one never regrets are one's mistakes."

——Oscar Wilde, *The Picture of Dorian Gray*

With memory set smarting like a reopened wound, a man's past is not simply a dead history, an outworn preparation of the present: it is not a repented error shaken loose from the life: it is a still quivering part of himself, bringing shudders and bitter flavors and the tinglings of a merited shame.

——George Eliot, *Middlemarch*

☆

"There is no refuge from memory and remorse in this world. The spirits of our foolish deeds haunt us, with or without repentance."

——Gilbert Parker, *Mrs. Falchion*

☆

"Youth is a blunder; Manhood a struggle; Old Age a regret."

——Benjamin Disraeli, *Coningsby*

☆

"Married in haste, we may repent at leisure."

——William Congreve, *The Old Bachelor*

☆

"We should regret our mistakes and learn from them, but never carry them forward into the future with us."

——Lucy Maud Montgomery, *Anne of Avonlea*

Sorrow

Sorrow comes in different levels, from a faint sense of sorrow at failing to find a beer in the refrigerator to the full-blown sense of sorrow at failing at love. Similar but carrying slightly less weight than the word "grief," sorrow is an emotion that sometimes tricks us into believing that it is something else, such as sadness, anger, weariness, pity or fear. Sorrow is a staple in literature, and there are a wide range of colorful descriptions to be found.

"When sorrows come, they come not single spies, But in battalions!"

—William Shakespeare, *Hamlet, Prince of Denmark*

There is no dealing with great sorrow as if it were under the control of our wills. It is a terrible phenomenon, whose laws we must study, and to whose conditions we must submit, if we would mitigate it.

—J. Sheridan Le Fanu, *Uncle Silas*

"I have read in your face, as plain as if it was a book, that but for some trouble and sorrow we should never know half the good there is about us."

——Charles Dickens, *The Haunted Man*

It was a long and gloomy night that gathered on me, haunted by the ghosts of many hopes, of many dear remembrances, many errors, many unavailing sorrows and regrets.

——Charles Dickens, *David Copperfield*

These bitter sorrows of childhood! when sorrow is all new and strange, when hope has not yet got wings to fly beyond the days and weeks, and the space from summer to summer seems measureless.

——George Eliot, *The Mill on the Floss*

Chapter 3

Things that
Make us Smile

Chapter 3
【微笑みを与えるもの】

微笑みは不安や緊張を緩和し、幸福感をもたらします。あなたが笑顔でいれば、周りの人たちも気持ちが和らぎ、場は喜びで満たされるでしょう。わたしたちが読んでいる本の中でも同じように、登場人物たちは彼らの世界に存在する動物の愛らしさや自然がつくり出す情景、聞こえてくる音によって幸せを感じ、微笑んでいるのです。

Vocabulary わからない語は巻末のワードリストで確認しましょう。

- [ ] badger
- [ ] witty
- [ ] merciful
- [ ] companion
- [ ] lovable
- [ ] fairy
- [ ] relish
- [ ] robin
- [ ] nostalgia
- [ ] optimism

Pick Up 名言の一部を和訳と共に読んで、含蓄を味わいましょう。

Cheerfulness and content are great beautifiers, and are famous preservers of youthful looks, depend upon it. (朗らかさと満足感は人を美しく見せ若々しい外見を保たせる、よく知られた特効薬であり、それは間違いのないことである) (⇒ p.51)

"Draw your chair up and hand me my violin, for the only problem we have still to solve is how to while away these bleak autumnal evenings." (きみの椅子を寄せて私のバイオリンをとっておくれ。私たちに残された仕事は、このもの寂しい秋の夜をいかに過ごすかということだけだからね) (⇒ p.61)

The day was made for laziness, and lying on one's back in green places, and staring at the sky till its brightness forced one to shut one's eyes and go to sleep. (その日は怠けるためにある日だった。緑地に寝ころび、まぶしくて目があけていられなくなるまで空を見つめ、やがて眠ってしまうような日だ) (⇒ p.64)

Animals

Animals play a large role in many books, especially those written for children. They are generally depicted as loyal and intelligent, and with the exception of Stephen King and writers of hunting adventures, it is difficult to find a writer who has anything bad to say about them. My favorite quote about animals does not come from literature, but I personally find it very amusing. It is, "Disneyland is a people trap set by a mouse."

All animals, except man, know that the principal business of life is to enjoy it.

—Samuel Butler, *The Way of All Flesh*

"Everything is made out of Magic, leaves and trees, flowers and birds, badgers and foxes and squirrels and people. So it must be all around us. In this garden—in all the places."

—Frances Hodgson Burnett, *The Secret Garden*

"I love them," said Dorothy. "They are so nice and selfish. Dogs are too good and unselfish. They make me feel uncomfortable. But cats are gloriously human."

—Lucy Maud Montgomery, *Anne of the Island*

"Nature teaches beasts to know their friends."

—William Shakespeare, *Coriolanus*

"Strange life a dog's," said Jolyon suddenly: "The only four-footer with rudiments of altruism and a sense of God!"

—John Galsworthy, *The Forsyte Saga*

Beauty

Beauty comes in many shapes and forms and has the ability to illuminate both animate and inanimate subjects. Although beautiful women are a staple for the main characters in literature, man has been describing stunning beauties since the beginning of time, and there is little left to say about them. Consequently, many of the best quotations tend to take a more cynical view of beauty, but despite this, they still seem to hit the nail on the head and provide food for thought.

"I'm afraid to speak or move for fear all this wonderful beauty will vanish just like a broken silence."

——Lucy Maud Montgomery, *Anne of the Island*

Cheerfulness and content are great beautifiers, and are famous preservers of youthful looks, depend upon it.

——Charles Dickens, *Barnaby Rudge*

"She behaves as if she was beautiful. Most American women do. It is the secret of their charm."

—Oscar Wilde, *The Picture of Dorian Gray*

She had once been described, by one who saw below the surface, as a perfectly beautiful woman in an absolutely plain shell.

—Florence L. Barclay, *The Rosary*

A witty woman is a treasure; a witty Beauty is a power.

—George Meredith, *Diana of the Crossways*

Books

In an essay entitled *Of Studies*, Sir Francis Bacon said, "Some books are to be tasted, others to be swallowed, and some few to be chewed and digested." Writers in general tend to believe that everything they write is to be "chewed and digested," even when, in the opinion of others, a simple taste is all that's needed. But, there is no shortage of people who believe that books are the greatest source of knowledge available to mankind, and the quotations below seem to agree with this point of view.

"I declare after all there is no enjoyment like reading! How much sooner one tires of anything than of a book!"

—Jane Austen, *Pride and Prejudice*

Books—the generous friends who met me without suspicion—the merciful masters who never used me ill!

—Wilkie Collins, *Armadale*

Each had his past shut in him like the leaves of a book known to him by heart; and his friends could only read the title.

—Virginia Woolf, *Jacob's Room*

❦

"When I am king, they shall not have bread and shelter only, but also teachings out of books; for a full belly is little worth where the mind is starved."

—Mark Twain, *The Prince and The Pauper*

❦

"The proper study of mankind is books."

—Aldous Huxley, *Crome Yellow*

Children and Childhood

Childhood is a period of innocence to which we can never return. The sense of curiosity, wonder and unconditional acceptance that children have is lost forever as we grow older. George Barnard Shaw once said, "Youth is wasted on the young," but I somehow get the feeling that adults would be even more efficient at wasting it. Literature generally places the blame for unpleasant personalities in children squarely on the shoulders of the parents, as can be seen from some of the following quotations.

"Mother says as th' two worst things as can happen to a child is never to have his own way—or always to have it. She doesn't know which is th' worst."

—Frances Hodgson Burnett, *The Secret Garden*

"Every time a child says, 'I don't believe in fairies,' there is a fairy somewhere that falls down dead."

—James M. Barrie, *Peter Pan*

We could never have loved the earth so well if we had had no childhood in it.

——George Eliot, *The Mill on the Floss*

Mother is the name for God in the lips and hearts of little children.

——William Makepeace Thackeray, *Vanity Fair*

The companions of our childhood always possess a certain power over our minds which hardly any later friend can obtain.

——Mary Shelley, *Frankenstein*

"My dear Watson, you as a medical man are continually gaining light as to the tendencies of a child by the study of the parents. Don't you see that the converse is equally valid. I have frequently gained my first real insight into the character of parents by studying their children."

——Sir Arthur Conan Doyle,
The Adventure of the Copper Beeches

Happiness

The whole world agrees that nothing can compete with happiness. Happiness is a cure for all types of ills, and, when consumed in sufficient quantities, it is the elixir of life. Happiness can be found all around us; the warmth of friendship in winter; the fragrance of fresh verdure in spring; the cool breezes of summer; the early morning mist in autumn. The pursuit of happiness is all-consuming, and surpasses even the pursuit of wealth.

There is no happiness like that of being loved by your fellow-creatures, and feeling that your presence is an addition to their comfort.

—Charlotte Brontë, *Jane Eyre*

I would always rather be happy than dignified.

—Charlotte Brontë, *Jane Eyre*

To me it seems that those who are happy in this world are better and more lovable people than those who are not.

—Samuel Butler, *The Way of All Flesh*

"Action may not always be happiness," said the general; "but there is no happiness without action."

—Benjamin Disraeli, *Lothair*

Anne was always glad in the happiness of her friends; but it is sometimes a little lonely to be surrounded everywhere by a happiness that is not your own.

—Lucy Maud Montgomery, *Anne of the Island*

"It is a poor heart that never rejoices."

—Charles Dickens, *Barnaby Rudge*

Laughter

Most people agree that nothing can beat a good laugh. Laughter washes the darkness from our souls and fills us with light. Research has proved that laughter has many health benefits. It reduces stress, helps to relieve pain, and it can enhance the body's level of immunity. Literature looks favorable on laughter. Many other concepts tend to be viewed from various angles, but as far as literature goes, laughter is a good thing and something to be encouraged.

Laughter and bitterness are often the veils with which a sore heart wraps its weakness from the world.

—H. Rider Haggard, *Cleopatra*

Laughter and tears are meant to turn the wheels of the same machinery of sensibility; one is wind-power, and the other water-power; that is all.

—Oliver Wendell Holmes, Sr.,
The Autocrat of the Breakfast Table

"You see, Wendy, when the first baby laughed for the first time, its laugh broke into a thousand pieces, and they all went skipping about, and that was the beginning of fairies."

——James M. Barrie, *Peter Pan*

"Life is a huge farce, and the advantage of possessing a sense of humour is that it enables one to defy fate with mocking laughter."

——George Gissing, *New Grub Street*

"For what do we live, but to make sport for our neighbours, and laugh at them in our turn?"

——Jane Austen, *Pride and Prejudice*

Music

Music, more than anything else, has the ability to reach the very depths of our soul. Music can make us shiver, give us gooseflesh, bring back happy (and sad) memories, and bring on the tears. Everybody has different tastes in music, but I've never met anybody who admitted to disliking it. My favorite quotation about music comes from conductor Leopold Stokowski, who said, "A painter paints pictures on canvas. But musicians paint their pictures on silence."

"Draw your chair up and hand me my violin, for the only problem we have still to solve is how to while away these bleak autumnal evenings."

——Sir Arthur Conan Doyle,
The Adventure of the Noble Bachelor

As hollow vessels produce a far more musical sound in falling than those which are substantial, so it will oftentimes be found that sentiments which have nothing in them make the loudest ringing in the world, and are the most relished.

——Charles Dickens, *Barnaby Rudge*

"Your voice and music are the same to me."

——William Makepeace Thackeray, *Vanity Fair*

"I think I should have no other mortal wants, if I could always have plenty of music. It seems to infuse strength into my limbs, and ideas into my brain. Life seems to go on without effort, when I am filled with music."

——George Eliot, *The Mill on the Floss*

By the cigars they smoke, and the composers they love, ye shall know the texture of men's souls.

——John Galsworthy, *The Forsyte Saga*

Nature

Nature, with its ability to stimulate and delight all of the five senses, is so glorious in its variety and scope that it is impossible to remain unmoved by it. Often we are so busy with our daily tasks and chores that we fail to notice the beauty of our surroundings, but what a profoundly satisfying experience it is to see the waves lapping on the sandy beach, the smell of freshly cut grass, the taste of freshly picked fruit, the sound of a lark at dawn, and the feel of a newborn puppy in our hands. Literature is generally in favor of nature, although the cruel, uncompassionate side of it that treats human life in the same way as it treats a fallen leaf is not overlooked.

Nothing in the world is quite as adorably lovely as a robin when he shows off—and they are nearly always doing it.

——Frances Hodgson Burnett, *The Secret Garden*

Sunlight is the life-blood of Nature. Mother Earth looks at us with such dull, soulless eyes, when the sunlight has died away from out of her. It makes us sad to be with her then; she does not seem to know us or to care for us.

—Jerome K. Jerome, *Three Men in a Boat*

The sky was a midnight-blue, like warm, deep, blue water, and the moon seemed to lie on it like a water-lily, floating forward with an invisible current.

—Willa Cather, *One of Ours*

The day was made for laziness, and lying on one's back in green places, and staring at the sky till its brightness forced one to shut one's eyes and go to sleep.

—Charles Dickens, *The Old Curiosity Shop*

A light wind swept over the corn, and all nature laughed in the sunshine.

—Anne Brontë, *The Tenant of Wildfell Hall*

It was one of those March days when the sun shines hot and the wind blows cold: when it is summer in the light, and winter in the shade.

—Charles Dickens, *Great Expectations*

"What's in a name?
That which we call a rose
By any other name would smell as sweet."

—William Shakespeare, *Romeo and Juliet*

Youth

We all look back on our youth with nostalgia and wish that we could return to those idyllic days when we knew what the underside of the table looked like and what soil tasted like. Long summer days that seemed to last forever, and the stamina to remain active for the entire day without needing sleep. But, the attractiveness of youth is probably better for lasting only a short period of time. Everything looks better with the benefit of hindsight. Humorist Dave Barry once said, "You can only be young once. But you can always be immature." I will therefore remain satisfied with my immaturity.

"You must pay the penalty of growing-up, Paul. You must leave fairyland behind you."

——Lucy Maud Montgomery, *Anne of the Island*

Youth is a failing only too easily outgrown.

——Agatha Christie, *The Secret Adversary*

Your tears come easy, when you're young, and beginning the world. Your tears come easy, when you're old, and leaving it.

—Wilkie Collins, *The Moonstone*

❧

Youth is like spring, an overpraised season.

—Samuel Butler, *The Way of All Flesh*

❧

Some twenty years her senior, he preserved a gift that she supposed herself to have already lost—not youth's creative power, but its self-confidence and optimism.

—E. M. Forster, *Howards End*

❧

"Young men want to be faithful, and are not; old men want to be faithless, and cannot."

—Oscar Wilde, *The Picture of Dorian Gray*

Chapter 4

Things that Make us Uncomfortable

Chapter 4
【不安を煽るもの】

あなたはどんなときに不安を感じるでしょうか？大事な予定を前に、失敗してしまうのではないかと恐れを抱く。その場の勢いでつい感情をぶつけたり、言い逃れをしたり見栄を張ったりして、後から悔やむこともあるでしょう。言葉で表すのが難しいこうした複雑な感情は紙一重で、作家たちは良い面も悪い面も見出しています。

Vocabulary わからない語は巻末のワードリストで確認しましょう。

- ☐ temper
- ☐ dusk
- ☐ narcissistically
- ☐ incongruous
- ☐ conceitful
- ☐ folly
- ☐ abhorrent
- ☐ secrecy
- ☐ self-deprecation
- ☐ anguish

Pick Up 名言の一部を和訳と共に読んで、含蓄を味わいましょう。

But often the great cat Fate lets us go only to clutch us again in a fiercer grip. (しかし偉大な猫である〈運命〉がしばしば私たちを釈放してくれるのは、ふたたびその爪でもっと強く私たちを捕らえるためである) (⇒ p.74)

The longest way must have its close, —the gloomiest night will wear on to a morning. (どれほど長い道にも必ず終点がある。どれほど暗い夜も朝までしか続かない) (⇒ p.79)

No insect hangs its nest on threads as frail as those which will sustain the weight of human vanity. (人間の虚栄心ほどの重ささか支えられない脆い糸の上には、どんな昆虫も巣を作らない) (⇒ p.85)

Anger

Anger features predominantly in literature, and it is displayed in all of its various shades, from the cute attempts at anger by young children through to the raging fury of very dangerous men. Being one of the strongest emotions alongside love, writers usually have great fun finding the most vivid phrases to describe it.

Angry people are not always wise.

—Jane Austen, *Pride and Prejudice*

"My tongue will tell the anger of my heart,
Or else my heart, concealing it, will break."

—William Shakespeare, *The Taming of the Shrew*

An angry skipper makes an unhappy crew.

—Rudyard Kipling, *Captains Courageous*

Yet if he upbraided her in his hurry, it was to repent bitterly his temper the next instant, and to feel its effects more than she, temper being a weapon that we hold by the blade.

——James M. Barrie, *The Little Minister*

When angry, count four; when very angry, swear.

——Mark Twain, *The Tragedy of Pudd'nhead Wilson*

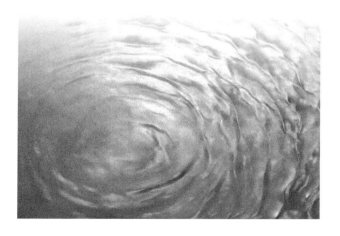

Destiny

The word "destiny" and "fate" are generally thought to be interchangeable and are used as such in literature in many cases, but they do have a slightly different nuance. The definition of destiny is, "a set of predetermined events within one's life that are the result of the decisions one has made," and the definition of fate is, "the preordained course of one's life that will occur regardless of the decisions one has made." In other words, we are responsible for our destinies, but our fates are out of our hands.

Destiny has a constant passion for the incongruous.

—Booth Tarkington, *The Magnificent Ambersons*

The future was with Fate. The present was our own.

—Sir Arthur Conan Doyle, *The Poison Belt*

But often the great cat Fate lets us go only to clutch us again in a fiercer grip.

—Sir Arthur Conan Doyle, *The Curse of Eve*

"What must be shall be."

—William Shakespeare, *Romeo and Juliet*

We sometimes had those little rubs which Providence sends to enhance the value of its favours.

—Oliver Goldsmith, *The Vicar of Wakefield*

Failure

Failure and success receive wide coverage at the hands of authors. And, in most cases, success is not achieved until a full dose of failure has been administered. Literature treats failure like a vaccine and success like good health. In other words, without an injection of failure to teach the body immunity, success will never come. In real life, of course, things are different. Maybe that is why literature is so captivating. It provides us with a tempting glimpse of the unattainable.

For, so inconsistent is human nature, especially in the ideal, that not to undertake a thing at all seems better than to undertake and come short.

——Harriet Beecher Stowe, *Uncle Tom's Cabin*

If success is rare and slow, everybody knows how quick and easy ruin is.

——William Makepeace Thackeray, *Vanity Fair*

"You will profit by the failure, and will avoid it

another time. I have done a similar thing myself, in construction, often. Every failure teaches a man something, if he will learn."

——Charles Dickens, *Little Dorrit*

"Next to trying and winning, the best thing is trying and failing."

——Lucy Maud Montgomery, *Anne of Green Gables*

"We learn from failure, not from success!"

——Bram Stoker, *Dracula*

Fear

Fear is our guardian angel. It prevents us from exposing ourselves to danger in all aspects of daily life, from cooking eggs and slicing apples through to crossing the road. It can also help us resist the temptation of making unwise investments. Despite this, fear is treated negatively in literature under normal circumstances. It is seen as something that is abhorrent and best avoided. The reason for this is because the antonym of "fear" is "courage." Maybe a more suitable antonym would be "recklessness."

Ignorance is the parent of fear.

——Herman Melville, *Moby Dick*

Fear makes us feel our humanity.

——Benjamin Disraeli, *Vivian Grey*

Something plucked at my heart and made me feel afraid.

——Algernon Blackwood, *The Willows*

Fear is a tyrant and a despot, more terrible than the rack, more potent than the stake.

—Edgar Wallace, *The Clue of the Twisted Candle*

Night, the mother of fear and mystery, was coming upon me.

—H. G. Wells, *The War of the Worlds*

The human brain is capable of only one strong emotion at a time, and if it be filled with curiosity or scientific enthusiasm, there is no room for fear.

—Sir Arthur Conan Doyle, *The Brown Hand*

Night

Night is a time of peace and tranquility, a time of sweetness and tenderness, but also a time of anguish and a time of fear. The night provides the ambience for romance, but also the shadows for spying, violence and murder. Fear of the dark is a primeval instinct, and authors are skilled at utilizing this fear to instill us with a sense of dread that will return to the front of our minds the next time we are out on a dark and silent night.

At the enchanted metropolitan twilight I felt a haunting loneliness sometimes, and felt it in others—poor young clerks who loitered in front of windows waiting until it was time for a solitary restaurant dinner—young clerks in the dusk, wasting the most poignant moments of night and life.

——F. Scott Fitzgerald, *The Great Gatsby*

The longest way must have its close, —the gloomiest night will wear on to a morning.

——Harriet Beecher Stowe, *Uncle Tom's Cabin*

The cool peace and dewy sweetness of the night filled me with a mood of hope: not hope on any definite point, but a general sense of encouragement and heart-ease.

—Charlotte Brontë, *Villette*

The lamp was burning dim and the first cold light of dawn was breaking through the window. The night had been long and dark but the day was the sweeter and the purer in consequence.

—Sir Arthur Conan Doyle, *The Curse of Eve*

"Good night, sweet prince, and flights of angels sing thee to thy rest!"

—William Shakespeare, *Hamlet, Prince of Denmark*

Pride

As can be seen from the quotations below, the word "pride" can be translated into Japanese as both "being proud," which generally has a positive meaning, and "being conceitful," which is less favorable. Pride is a noble emotion that affirms the accomplishments of you, your family, your peers, your country, and the significance of your existence while nourishing your desire to improve further, but in the wrong hands, it can quickly turn into an ugly, condescending attitude. In this sense, pride is a very dangerous emotion.

Poor nations are hungry, and rich nations are proud; and pride and hunger will ever be at variance.

——Jonathan Swift, *Gulliver's Travels*

"It is not the broken heart that kills, but broken pride, monseigneur."

——Gilbert Parker, *The Battle of the Strong*

"My pride fell with my fortunes."

——William Shakespeare, *As You Like It*

Pride is one of the seven deadly sins; but it cannot be the pride of a mother in her children, for that is a compound of two cardinal virtues—faith and hope.

——Charles Dickens, *Nicholas Nickleby*

"Proud people breed sad sorrows for themselves."

——Emily Brontë, *Wuthering Heights*

"Vanity and pride are different things, though the words are often used synonymously. A person may be proud without being vain. Pride relates more to our opinion of ourselves, vanity to what we would have others think of us."

——Jane Austen, *Pride and Prejudice*

Secrets

For some reason, the more important a secret is, the more we are tempted to divulge it. There are many idioms in most languages related to secrets, and English is no exception. A "skeleton in the closet," for example, is a family secret that is usually embarrassing, and "letting the cat out of the bag" means to unintentionally reveal a secret. This seems to indicate that secrecy plays an important role in our lives.

Never tell all you know—not even to the person you know best.

——Agatha Christie, *The Secret Adversary*

"There are no secrets better kept than the secrets everybody guesses."

——George Bernard Shaw, *Mrs. Warren's Profession*

Her heart lived in no cherished secrets of its own, but in feelings which it longed to share with all the world.

——George Eliot, *Adam Bede*

In all secrets there is a kind of guilt, however beautiful or joyful they may be, or for what good end they may be set to serve. Secrecy means evasion, and evasion means a problem to the moral mind.

——Gilbert Parker, *The Right of Way*

"Don't you think that any secret course is an unworthy one?"

——Charles Dickens, *David Copperfield*

Vanity

The dictionary defines vanity as "the quality or condition of being vain," but in most cases vanity is not judged on a personal level, but by others when we act narcissistically in public. Despite this, Christianity views vanity as a form of pride, which is one of the seven cardinal sins, so it is looked upon as a negative trait in literature. However, if we are to believe American essayist and critic Logan Pearsall Smith, authors tend to be more guilty of vanity than others: "Every author, however modest, keeps a most outrageous vanity chained like a madman in the padded cell of his breast."

"Had I been in love, I could not have been more wretchedly blind! But vanity, not love, has been my folly."

——Jane Austen, *Pride and Prejudice*

No insect hangs its nest on threads as frail as those which will sustain the weight of human vanity.

——Edith Wharton, *The House of Mirth*

Miss Bart was discerning enough to know that the inner vanity is generally in proportion to the outer self-depreciation.

——Edith Wharton, *The House of Mirth*

Our vanities differ as our noses do.

——George Eliot, *Middlemarch*

Vanity working on a weak head, produces every sort of mischief.

——Jane Austen, *Emma*

Chapter 5

Things that
We Want

Chapter 5
【手に入れたいもの】

教育によって身につけた知識や想像力は、あなたに夢や理想を抱かせます。年齢も限界もない真の友情や愛は、物事がうまくいかないときでもあなたに救いの手を差し伸べるでしょう。本章で語られているのは、お金を払って買うものではなく、心を豊かにする「人生の財産」と呼べるものであり、文学はそれを言葉で与えてくれます。

Vocabulary わからない語は巻末のワードリストで確認しましょう。

- [ ] curiosity
- [ ] confession
- [ ] intimacy
- [ ] sanctuary
- [ ] perception
- [ ] judicious
- [ ] versatility
- [ ] undaunted
- [ ] decorum
- [ ] self-reliance

Pick Up 名言の一部を和訳と共に読んで、含蓄を味わいましょう。

"There is no education like adversity." (逆境に勝る教育はない) (⇒ p.90)

"It's the people who try to be clever who never are; the people who are clever never think of trying to be." (賢くあろうとする者は決して賢くならない。賢い者は、決して賢い者になろうとはしない) (⇒ p.97)

"A lover without indiscretion is no lover at all. Circumspection and devotion are a contradiction in terms." (無分別なところのない恋人なんて、恋人ではありません。慎重さと熱愛は言葉のうえで相容れないものですよ) (⇒ p.105)

Education

Education is a true liberator. It provides us with knowledge and skills, fosters curiosity and creativity, and gives us the means to earn a living. There is a Chinese proverb that says, "Give a man a fish and feed him for a day. Teach a man to fish and feed him for life," which is quite similar to a George Eliot quotation that goes, "Better spend an extra hundred or two on your son's education, than leave it him in your will."

To learn one must be humble. But life is the great teacher.

—James Joyce, *Ulysses*

It being a part of Mrs. Pipchin's system not to encourage a child's mind to develop and expand itself like a young flower, but to open it by force like an oyster.

—Charles Dickens, *Dombey and Son*

"Better spend an extra hundred or two on your son's education, than leave it him in your will."

——George Eliot, *The Mill on the Floss*

꙳

Ignorance is the parent of fear.

——Herman Melville, *Moby Dick*

꙳

"If you exercise your mind, George, it will get hungry just as your body does."

——Louisa May Alcott, *Little Men*

꙳

"There is no education like adversity."

——Benjamin Disraeli, *Endymion*

Forgiveness

To err is human, to forgive is divine. So said Alexander Pope in *An Essay on Criticism*. This is, of course, true if one is forgiving an unintentional or inconsequential mistake, but forgiving an intentional deception or unsociable act is not quite as easy. People who are able to forgive another who has caused them serious grief or misfortune are few and far between. John F. Kennedy probably said it best when he said, "Forgive your enemies, but never forget their names."

It is so much easier to forgive a failure than a success.

—Charles Dudley Warner, *A Little Journey in the World*

"After a good dinner one can forgive anybody, even one's own relations."

—Oscar Wilde, *A Woman of No Importance*

"The quality of mercy is not strain'd,
It droppeth as the gentle rain from heaven
Upon the place beneath. It is twice blest,
It blesseth him that gives, and him that takes."

—William Shakespeare, *The Merchant of Venice*

It is a good rule in life never to apologize. The right sort of people do not want apologies, and the wrong sort take a mean advantage of them.

—P. G. Wodehouse, *The Man Upstairs*

He covered page after page with wild words of sorrow and wilder words of pain. There is a luxury in self-reproach. When we blame ourselves, we feel that no one else has a right to blame us. It is the confession, not the priest, that gives us absolution.

—Oscar Wilde, *The Picture of Dorian Gray*

Friendship

True friendship is hard to find, and those who manage it are fortunate indeed. In English we have the phrase, "fair weather friend." As this phrase implies, fair weather friends only stick around when the going is easy (i.e. when the weather is good). As soon as things get complicated (i.e. when the weather turns bad), they are gone. This is summed up in an anonymous quotation, which goes, "A real friend is one who walks in when the rest of the world walks out."

"It seems to me a most dreadful thing to go out of the world and not leave one person behind you who is sorry you are gone,"

—Lucy Maud Montgomery, *Anne of the Island*

"Friendship, I fancy, means one heart between two."

—George Meredith, *Diana of the Crossways*

"I love thee, Macumazahn, for we have grown grey together, and there is that between us that cannot be seen, and yet is too strong for breaking."

——H. Rider Haggard, *Allan Quatermain*

"It is not time or opportunity that is to determine intimacy;—it is disposition alone. Seven years would be insufficient to make some people acquainted with each other, and seven days are more than enough for others."

——Jane Austen, *Sense and Sensibility*

Imagination

Imagination provides us with a sanctuary in which we can escape the realities of daily life. It also provides us with an endless supply of dreams and ideals for a better life. Without imagination, the human race would be cultureless and bound by the limitations of the way we perceive reality. Albert Einstein summed this up admirably when he said, "I am enough of an artist to draw freely upon my imagination. Imagination is more important than knowledge. Knowledge is limited. Imagination encircles the world."

My imagination requires a judicious rein; I am afraid to let it loose, for it carries me sometimes into appalling places beyond the stars and beneath the world.

——Algernon Blackwood, *The Listener*

"I call people rich when they're able to meet the requirements of their imagination."

——Henry James, *The Portrait of a Lady*

Imagination is at the root of much that passes for love.

——Gilbert Parker, *The Trespasser*

"There are so many unpleasant things in the world already that there is no use in imagining any more."

——Lucy Maud Montgomery, *Anne of Avonlea*

You can't depend on your eyes when your imagination is out of focus.

——Mark Twain, *A Connecticut Yankee in King Arthur's Court*

Intelligence

Intelligence is difficult to define. We tend to believe that intelligence is synonymous with "wisdom" and "knowledge," but if we take a look at the synonyms provided for it in the thesaurus, we will find such words as "perception," "skill," "understanding" and "alertness." This seems to indicate that intelligence is not a result of education, but a natural ability spread in different quantities between all people. Albert Einstein once said, "Education is what remains after one has forgotten everything he learned in school," but maybe this should be changed to "Intelligence is what remains after one has forgotten everything he learned in school."

"It's the people who try to be clever who never are; the people who are clever never think of trying to be."

——Gilbert Parker, *The Battle of the Strong*

"Nature never appeals to intelligence until habit and instinct are useless. There is no intelligence where there is no change and no need of change."

——H. G. Wells, *The Time Machine*

"It is a law of nature we overlook, that intellectual versatility is the compensation for change, danger, and trouble."

——H. G. Wells, *The Time Machine*

Little things affect little minds.

——Benjamin Disraeli, *Sybil*

"I don't profess to be profound; but I do lay claim to common sense."

——Charles Dickens, *David Copperfield*

Knowledge

Knowledge is only useful when it is the correct knowledge, but sadly, the opinions of many people are based on incorrect knowledge. In his *An Essay on Criticism*, Alexander Pope said in 1709, "A little learning is a dangerous thing; drink deep, or taste not the Pierian spring." It neatly sums up the fact that only understanding half of a subject is worse than understanding nothing about it. In the modern age of the Internet and smartphones, knowledge is never further than a screen-tap away, so maybe we should get into the habit of double-checking all of our facts.

To be conscious that you are ignorant is a great step to knowledge.

—Benjamin Disraeli, *Sybil*

"As a general rule, the most successful man in life is the man who has the best information."

—Benjamin Disraeli, *Endymion*

Knowledge must be gained by ourselves. Mankind may supply us with facts; but the results, even if they agree with previous ones, must be the work of our own mind.

——Benjamin Disraeli, *The Young Duke*

"A baby has brains, but it doesn't know much. Experience is the only thing that brings knowledge, and the longer you are on earth the more experience you are sure to get."

——L. Frank Baum, *The Wonderful Wizard of Oz*

His knowledge was greater than his wisdom, and his powers were far superior to his character.

——Sir Arthur Conan Doyle, *The Leather Funnel*

Knowledge and timber shouldn't be much used, till they are seasoned.

——Oliver Wendell Holmes, Sr.,
The Autocrat of the Breakfast Table

Love

So much has been said about love that it is difficult to find something new to say. This has never stopped authors from continuing to concentrate on the subject, however. Literature generally views love as being a singular element that can only be given to one person. Love, however, comes in varying degrees and triggers different emotions depending on the recipient. It is quite possible for a man to love his wife, his children, his parents, his siblings, his dog, his car and soccer all at the same time. Humans have been blessed with unlimited supplies of love, and sharing it around does not dilute it in the least.

"I don't want sunbursts and marble halls. I just want you."

——Lucy Maud Montgomery, *Anne of the Island*

That which is loved may pass, but love hath no end.

——Gilbert Parker, *Parables of a Province*

"See how she leans her cheek upon her hand!
O that I were a glove upon that hand,
That I might touch that cheek!"

——William Shakespeare, *Romeo and Juliet*

Love is a flower that grows in any soil, works its sweet miracles undaunted by autumn frost or winter snow, blooming fair and fragrant all the year, and blessing those who give and those who receive.

——Louisa May Alcott, *Little Men*

"Love has no age, no limit; and no death."

——John Galsworthy, *The Forsyte Saga*

There are very few of us who have heart enough to be really in love without encouragement.

——Jane Austen, *Pride and Prejudice*

Manners

Good manners are as important as a good education and much cheaper. It costs nothing to be polite, to show compassion, to be punctual, or to treat others as you would like to be treated. Parents who instill manners into their children at an early age are providing them with a gift that will serve them well throughout their lives. One of my favorite quotes on this subject was by American philosopher Eric Hoffer, who said, "Rudeness is the weak man's imitation of strength."

"Unbidden guests
Are often welcomest when they are gone."

——William Shakespeare, *Henry VI, Part One*

No virtue could charm him, no vice shock him. He had about him a natural good manner, which seemed to qualify him for the highest circles, and yet he was never out of place in the lowest.

——Anthony Trollope, *Barchester Towers*

The world prefers decorum to honesty.

——George Meredith, *Diana of the Crossways*

But her correctness was of the finer sort, and had no air of being studied or achieved; conduct would never offer her a problem to be settled from a book of rules, for the rules were so deep within her that she was unconscious of them.

——Booth Tarkington, *Alice Adams*

"The great secret, Eliza, is not having bad manners or good manners or any other particular sort of manners, but having the same manner for all human souls: in short, behaving as if you were in Heaven, where there are no third-class carriages, and one soul is as good as another."

——George Bernard Shaw, *Pygmalion*

Passion

The word "passion" comes from the Latin term *passio* (suffering, obedience), and it was used to describe the suffering of Christ on the cross. It eventually came to mean "intense emotion," so lukewarm emotions are not included in the definition of the word. Writers often depict passionate lovers because they are more attractive to readers. Passion sells books, not mediocrity.

She was now forty years of age, childless, and with that inordinate passion for pleasure which is the secret of remaining young.

——Oscar Wilde, *Lord Arthur Savile's Crime*

"A lover without indiscretion is no lover at all. Circumspection and devotion are a contradiction in terms."

——Thomas Hardy, *The Hand of Ethelberta*

Picnics are very dear to those who are in the first stage of the tender passion.

——Sir Arthur Conan Doyle, *Our Derby Sweepstakes*

Passion takes no count of time; peril marks no hours or minutes; wrong makes its own calendar; and misery has solar systems peculiar to itself.

——Elizabeth Stuart Phelps, *The True Story of Guenever*

"Passion is like the lightning, it is beautiful, and it links the earth to heaven, but alas it blinds!"

——H. Rider Haggard, *Allan Quatermain*

It is an old prerogative of kings to govern everything but their passions.

——Charles Dickens, *The Pickwick Papers*

Respect

Communications are built on mutual respect. Everybody craves respect, and receiving it is as pleasant as receiving praise. Showing a lack of respect for a person, on the other hand, is likely to create an enemy. It is impossible to agree with everybody's opinions, but it is imperative to respect their right to have those opinions.

"I would not send a poor girl into the world, unarmed against her foes, and ignorant of the snares that beset her path; nor would I watch and guard her, till, deprived of self-respect and self-reliance, she lost the power or the will to watch and guard herself."

——Anne Brontë, *The Tenant of Wildfell Hall*

"The more things a man is ashamed of, the more respectable he is."

——George Bernard Shaw, *Man And Superman*

"Money is a needful and precious thing, and when well used, a noble thing, but I never want you to think it is the first or only prize to strive for. I'd rather see you poor men's wives, if you were happy, beloved, contented, than queens on thrones, without self-respect and peace."

——Louisa May Alcott, *Little Women*

Chapter 6

Things that
We Cannot Do Without

Chapter 6
【なくてはならないもの】

わたしたち人間は誕生から死ぬときまで、人生においてさまざまな出来事を経験します。その間に育まれる人格はそれぞれで、人と人との出会いが織りなす歴史のなかで、ときに寄り添いときにぶつかり合ってきました。「歴史は繰り返す」とはよく言ったものですが、下記の名言のように、その物語は世代を超えて紡がれていくのです。

Vocabulary わからない語は巻末のワードリストで確認しましょう。

- ☐ thought-provoking
- ☐ principle
- ☐ sincerity
- ☐ virtue
- ☐ sensation
- ☐ imbedded
- ☐ individual
- ☐ democracy
- ☐ embrace
- ☐ insight

Pick Up 名言の一部を和訳と共に読んで、含蓄を味わいましょう。

Events are as much the parents of the future as they were the children of the past. (数々の出来事は、それが過去の子どもであったように、未来の親でもある) (⇒ p.117)

Few people can resist doing what is universally expected of them. This invisible pressure is more difficult to stand against than individual tyranny. (多くの人々から期待されていることをせずにいられる人はほとんどいない。目に見えないこの重圧は、個々人から受ける圧迫よりも耐えがたい) (⇒ p.119)

It is familiarity with life that makes time speed quickly. When every day is a step in the unknown, as for children, the days are long with gathering of experience. (時の流れが早くなるのは、人生に慣れてしまったからである。子どもがそうであるように、毎日が未知の世界を進んでいく一歩であれば、経験を集めるために日々は長くなる) (⇒ p.129)

Birth

Birth is the greatest miracle. The emotions of the parents when a child is born are indescribable under most circumstances, and even writers have their limitations when it comes to putting this into words. Birth is therefore usually left as a foregone conclusion in literature, but it receives many indirect mentions. Sometimes, however, a writer can find a simile or metaphor that sums up birth in a thought-provoking manner. The words of Gilbert Parker, mentioned below, are a case in point.

When a child is born the mother also is born again.

——Gilbert Parker, *Parables of a Province*

"We are all born for love," said Morley. "It is the principle of existence, and its only end."

——Benjamin Disraeli, *Sybil*

The tree rustled. It had made music before they were born, and would continue after their deaths, but its song was of the moment.

—E. M. Forster, *Howards End*

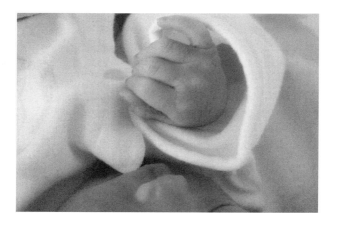

"I have heard it said that as we keep our birthdays when we are alive, so the ghosts of dead people, who are not easy in their graves, keep the day they died upon."

—Charles Dickens, *Barnaby Rudge*

Character

Descriptions of a bad character are always more fun to read than descriptions of a good character. It is as if a bad character provides writers with more scope to stretch their imagination in order to find the right metaphor for creating a perfect image in the reader's mind. On the surface, descriptions of bad characters are nothing more than insults, and a clever insult is always much more interesting than a clever word of praise.

She prized the frank, the open-hearted, the eager character beyond all others. Warmth and enthusiasm did captivate her still. She felt that she could so much more depend upon the sincerity of those who sometimes looked or said a careless or a hasty thing, than of those whose presence of mind never varied, whose tongue never slipped.

——Jane Austen, *Persuasion*

"The test of a man or woman's breeding is how they behave in a quarrel. Anybody can behave well when things are going smoothly."

——George Bernard Shaw, *The Philanderer*

If she did not wish to lead a virtuous life, at least she desired to enjoy a character for virtue.

—William Makepeace Thackeray, *Vanity Fair*

It is not true that suffering ennobles the character; happiness does that sometimes, but suffering, for the most part, makes men petty and vindictive.

—W. Somerset Maugham, *The Moon and Sixpence*

Dreams

Dreams are generally treated in two different ways in literature; either as something wonderful and inspiring, or as something that is fanciful and worthless. Personally, I opt for the former. In *The Alchemist*, Paulo Coelho said, "There is only one thing that makes a dream impossible to achieve: the fear of failure," and I like to believe that this is true.

"A dream itself is but a shadow."

—William Shakespeare, *Hamlet, Prince of Denmark*

It was a soft, reposeful summer landscape, as lovely as a dream, and as lonesome as Sunday.

—Mark Twain, *A Connecticut Yankee in King Arthur's Court*

How blessed are some people, whose lives have no fears, no dreads, to whom sleep is a blessing that comes nightly, and brings nothing but sweet dreams.

—Bram Stoker, *Dracula*

They who dream by day are cognizant of many things which escape those who dream only by night.

——Edgar Allan Poe, *Eleonora*

There is no more thrilling sensation I know of than sailing. It comes as near to flying as man has got to yet—except in dreams.

——Jerome K. Jerome, *Three Men in a Boat*

It was always the becoming he dreamed of, never the being.

——F. Scott Fitzgerald, *This Side of Paradise*

History

It is generally agreed that history teaches us how to avoid the same mistakes we made in the past, but there is still a lot of controversy over the accuracy of history as we know it. Sir Winston Churchill once said, "History is written by the victors," and if this is true, then we only have a biased view from one side of the real story. To a certain degree, Napoleon Bonaparte agreed with Churchill's opinion. He said, "History is the version of past events that people have decided to agree upon," which once again indicates that we are not in possession of the real truth.

Thus violent deeds live after men upon the earth, and traces of war and bloodshed will survive in mournful shapes long after those who worked the desolation are but atoms of earth themselves.

——Charles Dickens, *The Old Curiosity Shop*

Events are as much the parents of the future as they were the children of the past.

——John Galsworthy, *Saint's Progress*

All true histories contain instruction; though, in some, the treasure may be hard to find, and when found, so trivial in quantity, that the dry, shrivelled kernel scarcely compensates for the trouble of cracking the nut.

——Anne Brontë, *Agnes Grey*

"There are only two or three human stories, and they go on repeating themselves as fiercely as if they had never happened before; like the larks in this country, that have been singing the same five notes over for thousands of years."

——Willa Cather, *O Pioneers!*

Human Nature

Human nature is a fickle companion, in that certain parts of it are apt to change in accordance with each situation while others are deeply imbedded in human instinct and are impossible to change. The term "human nature" refers to the distinguishing characteristics that we all have independently of others, and we base our individual policies upon it in the hope that they will guide us successfully through life. We all think that we are doing others a favor by recommending that our own policies be adopted by everyone else in the whole world, but forcing them onto other people is the cause of many of the world's troubles.

"Revenge may be wicked, but it's natural."

——William Makepeace Thackeray, *Vanity Fair*

Few people can resist doing what is universally expected of them. This invisible pressure is more difficult to stand against than individual tyranny.

——Charles Dudley Warner, *That Fortune*

Cowardly dogs bark loudest.

——John Webster, *The White Devil*

"People do not like you to be different. If ever in your life you act differently from others, you will find it so, mademoiselle."

——John Galsworthy, *Saint's Progress*

Human nature is not obliged to be consistent.

——Lucy Maud Montgomery, *Anne's House of Dreams*

"I've never any pity for conceited people, because I think they carry their comfort about with them."

——George Eliot, *The Mill on the Floss*

There are people, who the more you do for them, the less they will do for themselves.

——Jane Austen, *Emma*

Justice

Justice is the oil that lubricates the mechanism of democracy. Not only does it discourage antisocial behavior, it also guarantees that everyone can receive a fair trial while having their human rights protected until proven either innocent or guilty. However, true justice is often nothing more than a dream for many people in the world. Winston Churchill once said, "The whole history of the world is summed up in the fact that, when nations are strong, they are not always just, and when they wish to be just, they are no longer strong." Let's see what literature thinks of justice.

Conscience is a coward, and those faults it has not strength enough to prevent, it seldom has justice enough to accuse.

——Oliver Goldsmith, *The Vicar of Wakefield*

Every human institution (justice included) will stretch a little, if you only pull it the right way.

——Wilkie Collins, *The Moonstone*

But injustice breeds injustice; the fighting with shadows and being defeated by them necessitates the setting up of substances to combat.

——Charles Dickens, *Bleak House*

"A book," I observed, "might be written on the Injustice of the Just."

——Anthony Hope, *Dolly Dialogues*

"There are times, young fellah, when every one of us must make a stand for human right and justice, or you never feel clean again."

——Sir Arthur Conan Doyle, *The Lost World*

Life

Life can be observed from various points of view; as the opposite of death, as a series of occurrences and experiences, and as a period of time to be either enjoyed or despised. All of these points of view are regularly covered in literature, and the way it is depicted can sometimes be inspiring. There is a recent trend in the United Kingdom to view funerals not as an opportunity for mourning the death of a person, but as a chance to celebrate that person's life. This is not a new concept, however. The famous children's author, Dr. Seuss, once said, "Don't cry because it's over, smile because it happened."

"Life is far too important a thing ever to talk seriously about."

——Oscar Wilde, *Lady Windermere's Fan*

Some of us rush through life, and some of us saunter through life. Mrs. Vesey sat through life.

——Wilkie Collins, *The Woman in White*

"There are two tragedies in life.
One is not to get your heart's desire. The other is to get it."

— George Bernard Shaw, *Man and Superman*

Remember to the last, that while there is life there is hope.

— Charles Dickens, *Wreck of the Golden Mary*

"Life is infinitely stranger than anything which the mind of man could invent."

— Sir Arthur Conan Doyle, *A Case of Identity*

Soul

The soul is said to represent the immortal essence of a person in many religions, and it has certainly been the target of philosophy for many years. Both Socrates and Plato were convinced that the soul continued to exist after death. This same philosophy is prevalent in Christianity, which believes that after death the soul is judged by God, who then determines whether it is to spend eternity in Heaven or Hell. Given that many authors who write in the English language have received a Christian upbringing, this point of view makes regular appearances in literature.

The absence of the soul is far more terrible in a living man than in a dead one.

—Charles Dickens, *Barnaby Rudge*

"Human beings, on the contrary, have a soul which lives forever, lives after the body has been turned to dust. It rises up through the clear, pure air beyond the glittering stars."

—Hans Christian Andersen, *The Little Mermaid*

"I don't like irony," she said; "it indicates a small soul."

——Edgar Rice Burroughs, *The Land That Time Forgot*

The voice of the sea speaks to the soul. The touch of the sea is sensuous, enfolding the body in its soft, close embrace.

——Kate Chopin, *The Awakening*

Beliefs must be lived in for a good while, before they accommodate themselves to the soul's wants, and wear loose enough to be comfortable.

——Oliver Wendell Holmes, Sr., *Elsie Venner*

Time

Time is often assigned two main roles in literature; one as poultice-like entity for curing disease, anger and grief, and the other as a malevolent entity whose sole objective is to cause problems for the human race by denying them sufficient leeway to complete a job or task. As to the former of these, Rose Kennedy, mother of former US president John F. Kennedy disagreed by saying, "It has been said, 'time heals all wounds.' I do not agree. The wounds remain. In time, the mind, protecting its sanity, covers them with scar tissue and the pain lessens. But it is never gone."

"My advice is, never do tomorrow what you can do today. Procrastination is the thief of time."

——Charles Dickens, *David Copperfield*

Time will explain.

——Jane Austen, *Persuasion*

You are here for but an instant, and you mustn't take yourself too seriously.

—Edgar Rice Burroughs, *The Land That Time Forgot*

"One event makes another: what we anticipate seldom occurs; what we least expected generally happens; and time can only prove which is most for our advantage."

—Benjamin Disraeli, *Henrietta Temple*

A moment's insight is sometimes worth a life's experience.

—Oliver Wendell Holmes, Sr.,
The Professor at the Breakfast Table

It is familiarity with life that makes time speed quickly. When every day is a step in the unknown, as for children, the days are long with gathering of experience.

——George Gissing, *The Private Papers of Henry Ryecroft*

"A person who has not done one half his day's work by ten o'clock, runs a chance of leaving the other half undone."

——Emily Brontë, *Wuthering Heights*

Word List

A

□ **abhorrent** 形 ひどくいやな

□ **ability** 名 ①できること, (〜する)
能力 ②才能

□ **above-ground** 副 地上[地表]に
[で]

□ **Abraham** 名 エイブラハム《人名》

□ **absence** 名 欠席, 欠如, 不在

□ **absolute** 形 ①完全な, 絶対の ②
無条件の ③確実な 名 絶対的なもの

□ **absolutely** 副 ①完全に, 確実に
②《yesを強調する返事として》そう
ですとも

□ **absolution** 名 ①〔義務などの〕免
除, 赦免 ②《キリスト教》罪の赦し

□ **accept** 動 ①受け入れる ②同意す
る, 認める

□ **acceptance** 名 ①受諾, 容認 ②
採用, 合格

□ **accident** 名 ①(不慮の)事故, 災
難 ②偶然

□ **accommodate** 動 ①収容する
②適合させる, 合わせる

□ **accomplished** 動 accomplish(成
し遂げる)の過去・過去分詞 形 ①完
成した ②(技量に)優れた, 熟達した

□ **accomplishment** 名 ①完成, 達
成 ②業績

□ **accordance** 名 一致, 適合 **in
accordance with** 〜に従って

□ **accountable** 形 ①《- for 〜》〜
に責任がある ②もっともな, 無理も
ない

□ **accuracy** 名 正確さ, 精度, 的確さ

□ **accuse** 動 《- of 〜》〜(の理由)で
告訴[非難]する

□ **accused** 動 accuse(告訴する)の
過去, 過去分詞 形 告発された, 非難
された

□ **achieve** 動 成し遂げる, 達成する,
成功を収める

□ **acquaint** 動 (〜を)熟知させる,
知り合いにさせる

□ **acquirement** 名 ①取得 ②〔獲得
した〕学識, 技能

□ **act** 名 行為, 行い 動 ①行動する ②
機能する ③演じる

□ **action** 熟 **take an action** 行動を取
る, 起こす

□ **active** 形 ①活動的な ②積極的な
③活動[作動]中の

□ **addition** 名 ①付加, 追加, 添加 ②
足し算

□ **administer** 動 ①管理する, 運営
する ②統治する ③施行する

- [ ] **admirably** 副 立派に, 見事に
- [ ] **admire** 動 感心する, 賞賛する
- [ ] **admiring** 形 感嘆する, 称賛の気持ちを表す
- [ ] **admit** 動 認める, 許可する, 入れる
- [ ] **adopt** 動 ①採択する, 選ぶ ②承認する ③養子にする
- [ ] **adorably** 副 愛らしく, かわいく
- [ ] **adult** 名 大人, 成人 形 大人の, 成人した
- [ ] **adultery** 名 姦通, 不倫, 不貞
- [ ] **adulthood** 名 大人 (adult) であること, 成人期
- [ ] **advancement** 名 進歩, 前進, 昇進
- [ ] **advantage** 名 有利な点 [立場], 強み, 優越
- [ ] **adventure** 名 冒険 動 危険をおかす
- [ ] **adversary** 名 敵, 対向者 形 敵の, 相手の
- [ ] **adversity** 名 ①逆境, 困難 ②困難 [不運] な出来事
- [ ] **advice** 名 忠告, 助言, 意見
- [ ] **affair** 名 ①事柄, 事件 ②《-s》業務, 仕事, やるべきこと
- [ ] **affect** 動 ①影響する ②(病気などが) おかす ③ふりをする 名 感情, 欲望
- [ ] **affirm** 動 断言する, 肯定する
- [ ] **after all** やはり, 結局
- [ ] **age** 熟 age of ～の時代 old age 老い, 老齢 (期)
- [ ] **aging** 名 ①老化, 高齢化 ②熟成 ③時効 形 ①年老いた ②老朽化した ③熟成した
- [ ] **agony** 名 苦悩, 激しい苦痛
- [ ] **agree with** (人) に同意する
- [ ] **ah** 間《驚き・悲しみ・賞賛などを表して》ああ, やっぱり
- [ ] **alas** 間 ああ《悲嘆・後悔・恐れなどを表す声》

- [ ] **Albert Einstein** アルベルト・アインシュタイン《ドイツ生まれのユダヤ人理論物理学者, 1879–1955》
- [ ] **alertness** 名 油断のないこと, 機敏さ
- [ ] **Alexander Pope** アレクサンダー・ポープ《18世紀イギリスの詩人で, 風刺詩やホメロスの翻訳で知られる, 1688–1744》
- [ ] **all** 熟 after all やはり, 結局 all right よろしい, 申し分ない all the time ずっと, いつも not ～ at all 少しも [全然] ～ない worst of all 一番困るのは, 最悪なことに
- [ ] **all-consuming** 形 すべてを費やす
- [ ] **all-encompassing** 形 あらゆるものを含む, ありとあらゆる
- [ ] **all-forgetfulness** 名 すっかり忘れていること
- [ ] **allow** 動 ①許す.《- … to ～》…が～するのを可能にする, …に～させておく ②与える
- [ ] **alongside** 副 そばに, 並んで 前 ～のそばに, ～と並んで
- [ ] **although** 接 ～だけれども, ～にもかかわらず, たとえ～でも
- [ ] **altruism** 名 利他主義
- [ ] **always** 熟 not always 必ずしも～であるとは限らない
- [ ] **ambience** 名〔ある場所が醸し出す独特の〕雰囲気, ムード
- [ ] **American** 形 アメリカ (人) の 名 アメリカ人
- [ ] **amount** 名 ①量, 額 ②《the –》合計 動 (総計～に) なる
- [ ] **amusing** 動 amuse (楽しませる) の現在分詞 形 楽しくさせる, 楽しい
- [ ] **An Essay on Criticism** 『批評論』《アレクサンダー・ポープ (Alexander Pope) が著した詩の一つ》
- [ ] **anchor** 名 ①いかり, アンカー ②(リレーなどの) 最終走者 [泳者], アンカー 動 停泊する [させる]

A
B
C
D
E
F
G
H
I
J
K
L
M
N
O
P
Q
R
S
T
U
V
W
X
Y
Z

- [ ] **and yet** それなのに, それにもかかわらず
- [ ] **angel** 名 ①天使 ②天使のような人
- [ ] **anger** 名 怒り 動 怒る, ～を怒らせる
- [ ] **angle** 名 ①角度 ②角
- [ ] **anguish** 名 〔精神的・肉体的な激しい〕苦痛, 苦悩
- [ ] **animate** 動 ①生気[元気]を与える ②アニメ化する 形 生きた, 活気のある
- [ ] **Anne** 名 アン《人名》
- [ ] **anonymous** 形 作者不明の, 匿名の
- [ ] **anticipate** 動 ①予期する ②先んじる
- [ ] **antisocial** 形 ①非社交的な, 愛想のない ②社会を乱す, 反社会的な
- [ ] **antonym** 名 《言語学》反意語
- [ ] **anxious** 形 ①心配な, 不安な ②切望して
- [ ] **anybody** 代 ①《疑問文・条件節で》誰か ②《否定文で》誰も (～ない) ③《肯定文で》誰でも **anybody who ～** する人はだれでも
- [ ] **anyone** 代 ①《疑問文・条件節で》誰か ②《否定文で》誰も (～ない) ③《肯定文で》誰でも
- [ ] **anything else** ほかの何か
- [ ] **apologize** 動 謝る, わびる
- [ ] **apology** 名 謝罪, 釈明
- [ ] **appalling** 形 恐ろしい, ぞっとさせる
- [ ] **appeal** 動 ①求める, 訴える ②(人の) 気に入る 名 ①要求, 訴え ②魅力, 人気
- [ ] **appear** 動 ①現れる, 見えてくる ②(～のように) 見える, ～らしい
- [ ] **appearance** 名 ①現れること, 出現 ②外見, 印象
- [ ] **append** 動 付け加える, 付け足す
- [ ] **appreciate** 動 ①正しく評価する, よさがわかる ②価値[相場]が上がる ③ありがたく思う
- [ ] **appreciative** 形 真価[良さ]が分かる, 鑑賞力のある
- [ ] **approach** 動 ①接近する ②話を持ちかける 名 接近, (～へ) 近づく道
- [ ] **apt** 形 《be - to ～》～しがちである, ～する傾向にある
- [ ] **arose** 動 arise (起こる) の過去
- [ ] **artist** 名 芸術家
- [ ] **as** 熟 **as far as** ～まで, ～する限り (では) ～に関しては, ～はどうかと言うと **as good as** ～も同然で, ほとんど **as if** あたかも～のように, まるで～みたいに **as long as** ～する限り, ～である限りは **as much as** ～と同じだけ **as soon as** ～するとすぐ, ～するや否や **as such** そのようなものとして **as to** ～に関しては, ～については **in the same way as [that]** ～～と同じように **just as** (ちょうど) であろうとおり **seen as** 《be - 》～として見られる **so long as** ～する限りは **such as** たとえば～, ～のような **such ～ as …** …のような～
- [ ] **ashamed** 形 恥じた, 気が引けた, 《be - of ～》～が恥ずかしい, ～を恥じている
- [ ] **aspect** 名 ①状況, 局面, 側面 ②外観, 様子
- [ ] **assign** 動 任命する, 割り当てる 名 譲り受け人
- [ ] **assuage** 動 ①〔苦しみや悲しみを〕和らげる, 緩和させる ②〔不安定なものを〕落ち着かせる, 鎮める
- [ ] **assume** 動 ①仮定する, 当然のことと思う ②引き受ける
- [ ] **at a time** 一度に, 続けざまに
- [ ] **at home** 自宅で, 在宅して
- [ ] **at last** ついに, とうとう
- [ ] **at least** 少なくとも
- [ ] **at leisure** ゆっくり, 暇で
- [ ] **at the root of** ～の根底に

132

- [ ] **at times** 時には
- [ ] **at work** 働いて, 作用して
- [ ] **atom** 名《物理》原子, アトム
- [ ] **attached** 動 attach (取りつける) の過去, 過去分詞 形ついている, 結びついた,《be – to ～》～に未練[愛着]がある
- [ ] **attack** 動①襲う, 攻める ②非難する ③(病気が)おかす 名①攻撃, 非難 ②発作, 発病
- [ ] **attempt** 動試みる, 企てる 名試み, 企て, 努力
- [ ] **attendance** 名①出席, 出席者数, 観客数 ②付き添い
- [ ] **attention** 名①注意, 集中 ②配慮, 手当て, 世話
- [ ] **attest** 動～が正しい[真である]と証明[断言]する
- [ ] **attitude** 名姿勢, 態度, 心構え
- [ ] **attractive** 形魅力的な, あいきょうのある
- [ ] **attractiveness** 名人を引き付ける[魅了する]こと
- [ ] **attribute** 動起因すると考える, (～の)せいにする 名特性, 属性
- [ ] **author** 名著者, 作家 動著作する, 創作する
- [ ] **autocrat** 名①[国家の]専制君主, 独裁者 ②[組織の]ワンマン, 支配者
- [ ] **autumnal** 形秋の
- [ ] **available** 形利用[使用・入手]できる, 得られる
- [ ] **avoid** 動避ける, (～を)しないようにする
- [ ] **Avonlea** 名アヴォンリー《地名》
- [ ] **awaken** 動①目を覚まさせる, 起こす, 目覚める ②《- to ～》～に気づく
- [ ] **away** 熟 **clear away** ～を片付ける, 取り払う **go away** 立ち去る **pass away** 過ぎ去る, 終わる
- [ ] **awfully** 副ひどく, たいへん悪く

B

- [ ] **bachelor** 名①独身男性 ②学士
- [ ] **back** 熟 **bring back** 戻す, 呼び戻す
- [ ] **bacon** 名ベーコン
- [ ] **bad luck** 災難, 不運
- [ ] **badge** 名バッジ, 記章
- [ ] **badger** 名アナグマ
- [ ] **bane** 名①致命傷, 破滅 ②死[破滅・苦しみ]のもと[原因]
- [ ] **bark** 名①ほえる声, どなり声 ②木の皮 動ほえる, どなる
- [ ] **Bart** 名バート《人名》
- [ ] **base** 名基礎, 土台, 本部 動《– on ～》～に基礎を置く, 基づく
- [ ] **based on**《be –》～に基づく
- [ ] **batchelour** 名①独身男性 ②[大学の学部を卒業した]学士 (= bachelor)
- [ ] **battalion** 名大隊, 軍勢
- [ ] **battle** 名戦闘, 戦い 動戦う
- [ ] **be out** 外出している
- [ ] **be over** 終わる
- [ ] **bear** 動①運ぶ ②支える ③耐える ④(子を)産む 名①熊 ②(株取引で)弱気
- [ ] **beast** 名①動物, けもの ②けもののような人, 非常にいやな人[物]
- [ ] **beat** 動①打つ, 鼓動する ②打ち負かす 名打つこと, 鼓動, 拍
- [ ] **beautifier** 名美化[美しく]する人[もの]
- [ ] **beautifully** 副美しく, 立派に, 見事に
- [ ] **beauty** 名①美, 美しい人[物] ②《the –》美点
- [ ] **beer** 名ビール
- [ ] **beginning** 動 begin (始まる)の現在分詞 名初め, 始まり
- [ ] **behave** 動振る舞う
- [ ] **behavior** 名振る舞い, 態度, 行動

A
B
C
D
E
F
G
H
I J
K
L
M
N
O
P
Q
R
S
T
U
V
W
X
Y
Z

133

□ **behind** 前 ①〜の後ろに, 〜の背後に ②〜に遅れて, 〜に劣って 副 ①後ろに, 背後に ②遅れて, 劣って **leave behind** あとにする, 〜を置き去りにする

□ **being** 動 be (〜である) の現在分詞 名 存在, 生命, 人間

□ **belief** 名 信じること, 信念, 信用

□ **believe in** 〜を信じる

□ **belly** 名 腹 動 ふくらます, ふくらむ

□ **beloved** 名 最愛の人 形 最愛の, いとしい

□ **below** 前 ①〜より下に ②〜以下の, 〜より劣る 副 下に［へ］

□ **beneath** 前 〜の下に［の］, 〜より低い 副 下に, 劣って

□ **benefit** 名 ①利益, 恩恵 ②〔失業保険・年金などの〕手当, 給付(金) 動 利益を得る, (〜の) ためになる

□ **beset** 動 ①〔しつこく〕〜を悩ませる［困らせる］②〈文〉〜を四方から攻撃する［襲う〕

□ **Betteredge** 名 ベタレッジ《人名》

□ **between A and B** AとBの間に

□ **beyond** 前 〜を越えて, 〜の向こうに 副 向こうに

□ **biased** 動 bias (偏見をもたせる) の過去, 過去分詞 形 偏見のある, 偏った, 先入観にとらわれた

□ **bill** 名 口, くちばし

□ **birth** 名 ①出産, 誕生 ②生まれ, 起源, (よい) 家柄

□ **bit** 動 bite (かむ) の過去, 過去分詞 名 ①小片, 少量 ②《a－》少し, ちょっと

□ **bitter** 形 ①にがい ②つらい 副 ①にがく ②ひどく, 激しく

□ **bitterly** 副 激しく, 苦々しく

□ **bitterness** 名 ①苦さ ②うらみ, 敵意

□ **blade** 名 ①(刀・ナイフなどの) 刃 ②(麦・稲などの) 葉

□ **blame** 動 とがめる, 非難する 名 ①責任, 罪 ②非難

□ **bleak** 形 荒涼とした, わびしい

□ **blend** 動 混合する, 溶け合う, 調和する 名 混合物

□ **blessed** 動 bless (祝福する) の過去, 過去分詞 形 祝福された, 恵まれた

□ **blesseth** 動 bless (祝福する) の三人称単数・現在 (=blesses)

□ **blessing** 動 bless (祝福する) の現在分詞 名 ①(神の) 恵み, 加護 ②祝福の祈り ③(食前・食後の) 祈り

□ **blest** 動 bless (祝福する) の過去, 過去分詞

□ **blind** 形 ①視覚障害がある, 目の不自由な ②わからない 動 ①目をくらます ②わからなくさせる

□ **bloodshed** 名 流血, 殺害, 虐殺

□ **blooming** 動 bloom (咲く) の現在分詞 形 花の咲いた, 花盛りの

□ **blow** 動 ①(風が) 吹く, (風が) 〜を吹き飛ばす ②息を吹く, (鼻を) かむ ③破裂する ④吹奏する 名 ①(風の) ひと吹き, 突風 ②(楽器の) 吹奏 ③打撃

□ **blunder** 名 大失敗, へま 動 へまをやらかす, やり損なう

□ **boldly** 副 大胆に, 厚かましく

□ **bondage** 名 奴隷状態, 束縛

□ **bore** 動 ①bear (耐える) の過去 ②退屈させる ③穴があく, 穴をあける 名 退屈な人［もの］, うんざりすること

□ **boredom** 名 退屈

□ **both A and B** AもBも

□ **bound** 動 ①bind (縛る) の過去, 過去分詞 ②跳びはねる ③境を接する, 制限する 形 ①縛られた, 束縛された ②《－ for 〜》〜行きの 名 境界(線), 限界

□ **brain** 名 ①脳 ②知力

□ **break into pieces** 粉々になる, 砕け散る

□ **break through** 〜を打ち破る

□ **breast** 名胸, 乳房 動(～を)胸に
受ける, 立ち向かう

□ **breath** 名①息, 呼吸 ②《a－》(風
の)そよぎ, 気配, きざし

□ **breathe** 動①呼吸する ②ひと息
つく, 休息する

□ **breed** 名品種, 血統 動①(動物が
子を)産む, 繁殖する ②(人が子を)
育てる

□ **breeding** 名①繁殖, 飼育 ②しつ
け, 教養, 育ち, 血統

□ **breeze** 名そよ風 動(風が)そよそ
よと吹く

□ **brick** 名レンガ, レンガ状のもの
形レンガ造りの

□ **brightness** 名①明るさ, 輝き ②
鮮やかさ ③聡明

□ **brilliant** 形光り輝く, 見事な, すば
らしい

□ **bring back** 戻す, 呼び戻す

□ **British** 形①英国人の ②イギリス
英語の 名英国人

□ **bully** 動いじめる, おどす 名いじ
めっ子

□ **burden** 名①荷 ②重荷 動荷[負
担]を負わす

□ **burning** 動burn (燃える)の現在
分詞 形①燃えている, 燃えるように
暑い ②のどが渇いた, 激しい

□ **busy with** 《be－》で忙しい

□ **but** 熟have no choice but to ～す
るしかない not ～ but … ～ではな
くて… nothing but ただ～だけ, ～
のほかは何も…ない

□ **by day** 昼間は, 日中は

□ **by far** はるかに, 断然

□ **by heart** 暗記して

□ **by no means** 決して～ではない

□ **by oneself** 自分だけで, 独力で

□ **by way of** ～のつもりで, ～のた
めに

C

□ **cabin** 名(丸太作りの)小屋, 船室,
キャビン

□ **cag'd** 形かごに入れられた(＝
caged)

□ **calendar** 名カレンダー, 暦

□ **call for** ～を求める, ～を呼び求め
る, 呼び出す

□ **calm** 形穏やかな, 落ち着いた 名
静けさ, 落ち着き 動まる, 静める

□ **can't** can (～できる)の否定形(＝
can not)

□ **candle** 名ろうそく

□ **cannot** can (～できる)の否定形(＝
can not)

□ **canvas** 名キャンバス地, ズック

□ **capable** 形①《be－of ～[～ing]》
～の能力[資質]がある ②有能な

□ **captain** 名長, 船長, 首領, 主将
動キャプテン[指揮官]を務める

□ **captivate** 動魅了する, とりこに
する

□ **captivating** 形人の心を捉える,
魅惑的な

□ **cardinal** 形①主要な ②深紅の,
緋色の 名①枢機卿 ②深紅色, 緋色

□ **care for** ～の世話をする, ～を気遣
う, ～を大事に思う

□ **careless** 形不注意な, うかつな

□ **carelessness** 名不注意, 軽率な
こと

□ **carriage** 名①馬車 ②乗り物, 車

□ **carry into** ～の中に運び入れる,
持ち込む

□ **celebrate** 動①祝う, 祝福する ②
祝典を開く

□ **cell** 名①細胞 ②小区分, 小室, 独房

□ **cellphone** 名携帯電話

□ **central** 形中央の, 主要な

□ **certain** 形①確実な, 必ず～する
②(人が)確信した ③ある ④いくら

135

かの 代 (〜の中の)いくつか

□ **certainly** 副 ①確かに, 必ず ② 《返答に用いて》もちろん, そのとおり, 承知しました

□ **change with** 〜とともに変化する

□ **chapter** 名 (書物の)章

□ **character** 名 ①特性, 個性 ②(小説・劇などの)登場人物 ③文字, 記号 ④品性, 人格

□ **characteristic** 形 特徴のある, 独特の 名 特徴, 特性, 特色, 持ち味

□ **charm** 名 ①魅力, 魔力 ②まじない, お守り 動 魅了する

□ **cheek** 名 ほお

□ **cheerfulness** 名 朗らかさ, 上機嫌

□ **cherish** 動 ①大切にする, (思い出などを)胸にしまっておく ②(アイデアなどを)温める ③(希望・イメージなどを)抱く

□ **chew** 動 ①かむ ②じっくり考える 名 かむこと, そしゃく

□ **chiefly** 副 主として, まず第一に

□ **childhood** 名 幼年[子ども]時代

□ **childless** 形 〔夫婦などが〕子どものいない

□ **Chinese** 形 中国(人)の 名 ①中国人 ②中国語

□ **choice** 名 選択(の範囲・自由), え り好み, 選ばれた人[物] **have no choice but to** 〜するしかない 形 精選した

□ **chore** 名 雑用, 雑役 動 雑用をする

□ **Christ** 名 イエス・キリスト (前4頃 –30頃)《キリスト教の始祖》間 しまった, ちくしょう

□ **Christian** 名 キリスト教徒, クリスチャン 形 キリスト(教)の

□ **Christianity** 名 キリスト教, キリスト教信仰

□ **cigar** 名 葉巻

□ **circle** 名 ①円, 円周, 輪 ②循環, 軌

道 ③仲間, サークル 動 回る, 囲む

□ **circumspection** 名 慎重さ, 用心

□ **circumstance** 名 ①(周囲の)事情, 状況, 環境 ②《-s》(人の)境遇, 生活状態

□ **civilization** 名 文明, 文明人(化)

□ **claim** 動 ①主張する ②要求する, 請求する 名 ①主張, 断言 ②要求, 請求

□ **clamour** 名 〈英〉①〔多くの人々の〕騒がしい声, 抗議の叫び ②〔自然現象・交通・楽器などの〕騒々しい音(= clamor)

□ **classified** 動 classify (分類する)の過去, 過去分詞 形 ①分類された ②機密の 名 ①(求人・不動産などの)広告(= classified ad) ②機密

□ **clear** 形 ①はっきりした, 明白な ②澄んだ ③(よく)晴れた 動 ①はっきりさせる ②片づける ③晴れる **clear away** 〜を取り除く, 取り払う 副 ①はっきりと ②すっかり, 完全に

□ **clerk** 名 事務員, 店員

□ **clever** 形 ①頭のよい, 利口な ②器用な, 上手な

□ **closer and closer** どんどん近づく

□ **closet** 名 戸棚, 物置, 押し入れ

□ **clothe** 動 服を着せる, 《受け身形で》(〜を)着ている, (〜の)格好をする

□ **clue** 名 手がかり, 糸口

□ **clumsy** 形 ぎこちない, 不器用な

□ **clutch** 動 ぐいっとつかむ, しっかり握る 名 ①つかむこと, しっかり握ること ②クラッチ

□ **cockerel** 名 ①若いおんどり[雄のニワトリ] ②〈俗〉〔生意気な〕若者, 若造

□ **cognizant** 形 《be - of 〜》〜に気付いている, 〜を知っている

□ **colorful** 形 ①カラフルな, 派手な ②生き生きとした

□ **combat** 名 戦闘 動 戦う, 効果がある

□ **come in** 〜の形で提供される，〜の形式がある

□ **come into** 〜に入ってくる

□ **come to life** 目覚める，復活する

□ **come up with** 〜を思いつく，考え出す，見つけ出す

□ **come upon** （人）に偶然出合う，〜を見つける

□ **comfort** 图①快適さ，満足 ②慰め ③安楽 動心地よくする，ほっとさせる，慰める

□ **comfortable** 形快適な，心地いい

□ **commit** 動①委託する ②引き受ける ③（罪などを）犯す

□ **commitment** 图委託，約束，確約，責任

□ **communication** 图伝えること，伝導，連絡

□ **companion** 图①友，仲間，連れ ②添えもの，つきもの

□ **companionship** 图（親密な）交わり，親交，友好

□ **compassion** 图思いやり，深い同情

□ **compassionate** 形思いやりのある，慈悲深い，心の優しい

□ **compensate** 動①補う ②補償する，補正する

□ **compensation** 图補償［賠償］金，埋め合わせ，補償

□ **compete** 動①競争する ②（競技に）参加する ③匹敵する

□ **complete** 形完全な，まったくの，完成した 動完成させる

□ **completely** 副完全に，すっかり

□ **complicated** 動complicate（複雑にする）の過去，過去分詞 形①複雑な ②むずかしい，困難な

□ **composer** 图作曲家，作者

□ **compound** 形合成の，複合の 图合成物，化合物，複合物 動混ぜ合わせる，合成する

□ **conceal** 動隠す，秘密にする

□ **conceit** 图うぬぼれ，自負心

□ **conceitful** 形非常にうぬぼれた，高慢な

□ **conceive** 動思いつく，心に抱く

□ **concentrate** 動一点に集める［集まる］，集中させる［する］

□ **concept** 图①概念，観念，テーマ ②（計画案などの）基本的な方向

□ **conclusion** 图結論，結末

□ **condescending** 形〔態度・話し方などが下の者に対して〕見下すような，偉そうな，横柄な

□ **condition** 图①（健康）状態，境遇 ②《-s》状況，様子 ③条件 動適応させる，条件づける

□ **conduct** 動①行い，振る舞い ②指導，指揮 動①指導する ②実施する，処理［処置］する

□ **conductor** 图指導者，案内者，管理者，指揮者，車掌

□ **confess** 動（隠し事などを）告白する，打ち明ける，白状する

□ **confession** 图告白，自白

□ **confidence** 图自信，確信，信頼，信用度

□ **confirm** 動確かめる，確かにする

□ **confused** confuse（混同する）の過去，過去分詞 形困惑した，混乱した

□ **connotation** 图〔文字どおりの意味に加えられる〕言外の意味，含み，含意

□ **conscience** 图良心

□ **conscious** 形①（状況などを）意識している，自覚している ②意識のある 图意識

□ **consequence** 图結果，成り行き

□ **consequently** 副したがって，結果として

□ **consider** 動①考慮する，〜しようと思う ②（〜と）みなす ③気にかけ

る, 思いやる

□ **consist** 動 ①《 – of ～》(部分・要素から) 成る ②《 – in ～》～に存在する, ～にある

□ **consistent** 形 首尾一貫した, 筋の通った, しっかりした

□ **constant** 形 ①絶えない, 一定の, 不変の ②不屈の, 確固たる 名 定数

□ **construction** 名 構造, 建設, 工事, 建物

□ **consume** 動 ①消費する, 費やす ②消滅させる ③摂取する ④夢中にさせる

□ **contain** 動 ①含む, 入っている ②(感情などを) 抑える

□ **contemplate** 動 ①熟考する, よく検討する ②じっと見つめる

□ **content** 名 ①《-s》中身, 内容, 目次 ②満足 形 満足して 動 満足する[させる]

□ **contented** 動 content (満足する) の過去, 過去分詞 形 満足した

□ **contentedly** 副 満足そうに

□ **context** 名 文脈, 前後関係, コンテクスト

□ **continually** 副 継続的に, 絶えず, ひっきりなしに

□ **contradict** 動 矛盾する, 否定する, 反論する

□ **contradiction** 名 ①否定, 反対 ②矛盾

□ **contrary** 形 反対の, 逆の 名 逆 **on the contrary** 逆に, それどころか 副 (～に) 反して, 逆らって

□ **control** 動 ①管理[支配]する ②抑制する, コントロールする 名 ①管理, 支配(力) ②抑制

□ **controversy** 名 論争, 議論

□ **conversation** 名 会話, 会談

□ **converse** 動 (打ち解けて) 話す, 会話する ①談話 名 ①談話 ②正反対, 逆 形 逆の, 正反対の

□ **conversely** 副 反対に, 逆に言えば

□ **convinced** 動 convince (納得させる) の過去, 過去分詞 形 確信した

□ **cooking** 動 cook (料理する) の過去, 過去分詞 名 料理(法), クッキング

□ **cool down** 冷ます, 涼しくする

□ **copper** 名 銅, 銅貨 動 銅で覆う, 銅板を貼る 形 銅の, 銅製の

□ **corn** 名 トウモロコシ, 穀物

□ **correct** 形 正しい, 適切な, りっぱな 動 (誤りを) 訂正する, 直す

□ **correctness** 名 正しさ, 正確さ

□ **cost** 名 ①値段, 費用 ②損失, 犠牲 動 (金・費用が) かかる, (～を) 要する, (人に金額を) 費やさせる

□ **could** 動 **If +《主語》+ could ～** できればなあ《仮定法》**could have done** ～だったかもしれない《仮定法》

□ **count** 動 ①数える ②(～を…と) みなす ③重要[大切]である 名 計算, 総計, 勘定

□ **courage** 名 勇気, 度胸

□ **courageous** 形 勇気のある

□ **course** 熟 **of course** もちろん, 当然

□ **court** 名 ①中庭, コート ②法廷, 裁判所 ③宮廷, 宮殿

□ **courtship** 名 ①求婚, 〔結婚を目的とした〕求愛 ②求婚期間, 〔結婚までの〕交際期間

□ **cover** 動 ①覆う, 包む, 隠す ②扱う, (～に) わたる, 及ぶ ③代わりを務める ④補う 名 覆い, カバー

□ **coverage** 名 ①取材範囲, 報道 ②保険による保護, 適用[通用]範囲

□ **covetousness** 名 強欲, 熱望

□ **coward** 名 臆病者 形 勇気のない, 臆病な

□ **cowardly** 形 臆病な 副 臆病に, 卑怯にも

□ **crack** 名 ①割れ目, ひび ②(裂けるような) 鋭い音 動 ①ひびが入る,

ひびを入れる, 割れる, 割る ②鈍い
音を出す

- □ **cranky** 形①〈話〉〔人が〕不機嫌な, 怒りっぽい, 気難しい・奇妙な ②〈話〉〔人が〕風変わり〔気まぐれ・奇妙〕な
- □ **crave** 動切望する
- □ **create** 動創造する, 生み出す, 引き起こす
- □ **creative** 形創造力のある, 独創的な
- □ **creativity** 名創造性, 独創力
- □ **creature** 名(神の)創造物, 生物, 動物
- □ **creeping** 形コソコソ取り入る, こびへつらう
- □ **crew** 名クルー, 乗組員, 搭乗員
- □ **crime** 名①(法律上の)罪, 犯罪 ②悪事, よくない行為
- □ **critic** 名批評家, 評論家, 批判をする人
- □ **criticism** 名批評, 非難, 反論, 評論
- □ **crossing** 動cross(横切る)の過去, 過去分詞 名横断, 交差点, 横断歩道, 踏み切り
- □ **crow** 名カラス(烏)
- □ **crowd** 動群がる, 混雑する 名群集, 雑踏, 多数, 聴衆
- □ **cruel** 形残酷な, 厳しい
- □ **cultureless** 形文化のない
- □ **cure** 名治療, 治癒, 矯正 動治療する, 矯正する, 取り除く
- □ **curiosity** 名①好奇心 ②珍しい物〔存在〕
- □ **curious** 形好奇心の強い, 珍しい, 奇妙な, 知りたがる
- □ **current** 形現在の, 目下の, 通用〔流通〕している 名流れ, 電流, 風潮
- □ **curse** 動のろう, ののしる 名のろい(の言葉), 悪態
- □ **cut** 熟short cut 近道
- □ **cynical** 形皮肉な, 冷笑的な, ひねくれた

D

- □ **daily** 形毎日の, 日常の 副毎日, 日ごとに
- □ **dancing** 動dance(踊る)の現在分詞 名ダンス, 舞踏
- □ **dare** 動《 – to 》思い切って[あえて]〜する 助思い切って[あえて]〜する 名挑戦
- □ **darkness** 名暗さ, 暗やみ
- □ **Dave Barry** デイヴ・バリー《アメリカのユーモア作家・コラムニスト, 1947–》
- □ **dawn** 名①夜明け ②《the – 》初め, きざし 動①(夜が)明ける ②(真実などが)わかり始める
- □ **day** 熟by day 昼間は, 日中は every day 毎日 these days このごろ
- □ **deadly** 形命にかかわる, 痛烈な, 破壊的な 副ひどく, 極度に
- □ **deal** 動①分配する ②《 – with〔in〕 》〜を扱う 名①取引, 扱い ②(不特定の)量, 額 a good〔great〕deal (of 〜) かなり〔ずいぶん・大量〕(の〜), 多額(の〜)
- □ **dealing** 名①取引, 対処 ②〔他人に対する〕振る舞い
- □ **dear to** (人)にとって大切な
- □ **death** 名①死, 死ぬこと ②《the –》終えん, 消滅
- □ **debate** 動①討論する ②思案する 名討論, ディベート
- □ **deception** 名だますこと, 詐欺
- □ **decide to do** 〜することに決める
- □ **decided** decide(決定する)の過去, 過去分詞 形はっきりした, 断固とした
- □ **decision** 名①決定, 決心 ②判決
- □ **declare** 動①宣言する ②断言する ③(税関で)申告する
- □ **decline** 動①断る ②傾く ③衰える 名①傾くこと ②下り坂, 衰え, 衰退

A
B
C
D
E
F
G
H
I
J
K
L
M
N
O
P
Q
R
S
T
U
V
W
X
Y
Z

□ **decorum** 図礼儀正しさ, 上品さ

□ **dedication** 図装飾

□ **deed** 図行為, 行動

□ **deeply** 副深く, 非常に

□ **defeat** 動①打ち破る, 負かす ②だめにする 図①敗北 ②挫折

□ **define** 動①定義する, 限定する ②〜の顕著な特性である

□ **definite** 形限定された, 明確な, はっきりした

□ **definition** 図定義, 限定

□ **defy** 動①拒む, 反抗する ②《 – +人 + to 〜》…に〜しろと挑む

□ **degree** 図①程度, 階級, 位, 身分 ②(温度・角度の) 度

□ **delight** 動喜ぶ, 喜ばす, 楽しむ, 楽しませる 図喜び, 愉快

□ **delusion** 図①〔判断力などを〕欺くこと, だますこと ②誤った信念〔考え・意見〕, 思いこみ

□ **democracy** 図民主主義, 民主政治

□ **Denmark** 図デンマーク《国名》

□ **denominator** 図①(分数の) 分母 ②共通の特徴, (好みなどの) 基準

□ **dent** 動①〔物を〕へこませる ②〔人の評判などを〕傷つける, おとしめる

□ **deny** 動否定する, 断る, 受けつけない

□ **depend** 動《 – on〔upon〕〜》①〜を頼る, 〜をあてにする ②〜による, 〜しだいである

□ **dependable** 形頼りになる, あてになる

□ **depict** 動①描写する ②言葉で表す, 伝える

□ **deprived** 動 deprive (奪う) の過去, 過去分詞 形恵まれない, 困窮している

□ **depth** 図深さ, 奥行き, 深いところ

□ **describe** 動 (言葉で) 描写する, 特色を述べる, 説明する

□ **description** 図 (言葉で) 記述 (すること), 描写 (すること)

□ **desert** 図砂漠, 不毛の地 形砂漠の, 人の住まない 動見捨てる

□ **desire** 動強く望む, 欲する 図欲望, 欲求, 願望

□ **desolation** 図荒廃, 荒れ地

□ **despair** 動絶望する, あきらめる 図絶望, 自暴自棄

□ **despicable** 形〔人の行為が〕見下げはてた, 卑劣な

□ **despise** 動軽蔑する

□ **despite** 前〜にもかかわらず

□ **despot** 図専制君主, 独裁者, 暴君

□ **destiny** 図運命, 宿命

□ **detect** 動見つける

□ **determine** 動①決心する〔させる〕②決定する〔させる〕③測定する

□ **develop** 動①発達する〔させる〕②開発する

□ **devoted** 動 devote (捧げる) の過去, 過去分詞 形献身的な, 熱心な, 愛情深い

□ **devotion** 図献身, 没頭, 忠誠

□ **dewy** 形①露にぬれた ②《詩》露のように新鮮な〔爽やかな・清らかな〕

□ **dialogue** 図対話, 話し合い

□ **dictionary** 図辞書, 辞典

□ **die of** 〜がもとで死ぬ

□ **die upon** 〜で死ぬ

□ **differ** 動異なる, 違う, 意見が合わない

□ **differently** 副 (〜と) 異なって, 違って

□ **digest** 動①消化する ②要約する 図①要約, ダイジェスト ②消化

□ **dignified** 動 dignify (威厳を付ける) の過去, 過去分詞 形威厳のある, 尊厳のある

□ **dignity** 図威厳, 品位, 尊さ, 敬意

□ **dilute** 動①薄くなる, 薄める ②弱くなる, 弱める 形 (色が) 薄い, さめた

140

□ **dim** 形 薄暗い, 見にくい

□ **direction** 名 ①方向, 方角 ②《-s》指示, 説明書 ③指導, 指揮 **in the direction of** ～の方向に

□ **disagree** 動 異議を唱える, 反対する

□ **disappointment** 名 失望

□ **discern** 動 見分ける, 識別する

□ **discourage** 動 ①やる気をそぐ, 失望させる ②《～するのを》阻止する, やめさせる

□ **disease** 名 ①病気 ②（社会や精神の）不健全な状態

□ **dishonour** 名 ①不名誉, 侮辱, 恥 ②軽蔑, 無礼 (= dishonor)

□ **dislike** 動 嫌う 名 反感, いや気

□ **dismal** 形 気の滅入る, 陰気な

□ **Disneyland** 名 ディズニーランド

□ **display** 動 展示する, 示す 名 展示, 陳列, 表出

□ **disposition** 名 ①気質, 気持ち ②配置, 配列

□ **disregard** 動 ①注意を払わない, 無視する ②軽視する, なおざりにする 名 無視, 軽視, 無関心

□ **distinguishing** 動 distinguish（見分ける）の現在分詞 形 特徴的な

□ **distrust** 名 不信, 疑惑 動 疑う, 不信感を抱く

□ **divine** 形 神聖な, 神の 名 《the D-》神

□ **divulge** 動 〔秘密などを〕漏らす, 打ち明ける, 暴露する

□ **do without** ～なしですませる

□ **doing** 動 do（～をする）の現在分詞 **enjoy doing** ～するのが好きだ, ～するのを楽しむ **go doing** ～をしに行く 名 ①すること, したこと ②《-s》行為, 出来事

□ **done** 熟 **could have done** ～だったかもしれない《仮定法》

□ **Dorothy** 名 ドロシー《人名》

□ **dose** 名 （薬剤の）1回の服用量

□ **doth** 動 do（～をする）の三人称単数・現在形 (= does)

□ **double-check** 動 〔作成した情報などに間違いがないように〕二重のチェックをする, 念のために再確認する

□ **down** 熟 **cool down** 冷ます, 涼しくする **fall down** 落ちる, ひっくり返る **put A down to B** AをBのせいにする, Aの対象をBに絞る

□ **Dr.** 名 ～博士,《医者に対して》～先生

□ **Dr. Seuss** ドクター・スース《アメリカの絵本作家・児童文学作家。本名はセオドア・スース・ガイゼル (Theodor Seuss Geisel), 1904–1991》

□ **draught** 名 〈英〉①〔部屋などの冷たい〕隙間風 ②〔煙突などの〕通気, 通風 ③〈文〉〔空気や飲み物を〕飲む［吸う］こと, 一飲み, 1回分 (= draft)

□ **draw** 動 ①引く, 引っ張る ②描く ③引き分けになる［する］

□ **dread** 動 恐れる, こわがる 名 恐怖, 不安

□ **dreadful** 形 恐ろしい

□ **dream of** ～を夢見る

□ **drift** 動 漂う 名 漂流

□ **droppeth** 動 drop（落ちる, 降る）の三人称単数・現在形 (= drops)

□ **duke** 名 公爵

□ **dull** 形 退屈な, 鈍い, くすんだ, ぼんやりした 動 鈍くなる［する］

□ **dullard** 名 愚か者, 頭の鈍い人, 物分かりの悪い人

□ **dunghill** 名 〔動物の〕糞の山, 肥溜

□ **dusk** 名 夕闇, 薄ã暗がり 形 暮れかかった, 薄暗い

□ **dust** 名 ちり, ほこり, ごみ, 粉 動 ちり［ほこり］を払う

□ **duty** 名 ①義務（感）, 責任 ②職務, 任務, 関税

□ **dying** 動 die（死ぬ）の現在分詞 形 死にかかっている, 消えそうな

141

E

- [ ] **e-mail** 名 電子メール 動 電子メールを[で]送る
- [ ] **each other** お互いに
- [ ] **eager** 形 ①熱心な ②《be – for ~》~を切望している，《be – to ~》しきりに~したがっている
- [ ] **eagerness** 名 熱心，熱望
- [ ] **earn** 動 ①儲ける，稼ぐ ②(名声を)博す
- [ ] **earnest** 名 熱心，真剣 形 熱心な，真剣な，重大な
- [ ] **earth** 熟 on earth 地球上で，この世で
- [ ] **earthquake** 名 地震，大変動
- [ ] **easily** 副 ①容易に，たやすく，苦もなく ②気楽に
- [ ] **education** 名 教育，教養
- [ ] **effect** 名 ①影響，効果，結果 ②実施，発効 動 もたらす，達成する
- [ ] **efficient** 形 ①効率的な，有効な ②有能な，敏腕な
- [ ] **effort** 名 努力(の成果)
- [ ] **either A or B** A かそれとも B
- [ ] **element** 名 要素，成分，元素
- [ ] **elixir** 名 ①不老不死の薬 ②万能薬
- [ ] **Eliza** 名 イライザ，エリザ《人名，通例 Elizabeth という女性の愛称》
- [ ] **else** 熟 anything else ほかの何か　no one else 他の誰一人として~しない　or else さもないと
- [ ] **embarrassing** 動 embarrass (恥ずかしい思いをさせる)の現在分詞 形 恥ずかしい，きまりが悪い，当惑させる
- [ ] **embarrassment** 名 当惑，困惑，きまり悪さ
- [ ] **embrace** 動 抱き締める 名 抱擁
- [ ] **emotion** 名 感激，感動，感情
- [ ] **employ** 動 ①(人を)雇う，使う ②利用する 名 雇用，職業

- [ ] **enable** 動 (~することを)可能にする，容易にする
- [ ] **enchanted** 形 魅惑の，魅了するような
- [ ] **encircle** 動 ~を取り巻く，取り囲む
- [ ] **encourage** 動 ①勇気づける ②促進する，助長する
- [ ] **encouragement** 名 激励，励み，促進
- [ ] **end** 熟 in the end とうとう，結局，ついに
- [ ] **endless** 形 終わりのない，無限の
- [ ] **endow** 動 〔神・自然などが人に資質・才能などを〕授ける，与える
- [ ] **endurance** 名 忍耐，我慢，耐久性
- [ ] **endure** 動 ①我慢する，耐え忍ぶ ②持ちこたえる
- [ ] **enemy** 名 敵
- [ ] **enfold** 動 くるむ，包む
- [ ] **enhance** 動 向上させる，価値を高める
- [ ] **enjoy doing** ~するのが好きだ，~するのを楽しむ
- [ ] **enjoyment** 名 楽しむこと，喜び
- [ ] **ennoble** 動 〔人格・品性などを〕高める，気高くする，高尚にする
- [ ] **enough of** ~はもうたくさん，十分だ
- [ ] **enough to do** ~するのに十分な
- [ ] **enthusiasm** 名 情熱，熱意，熱心
- [ ] **entire** 形 全体の，完全な，まったくの
- [ ] **entitle** 動 ①~に資格・権利を与える ②~に題名をつける，表題をつける
- [ ] **entity** 名 実在する物，実体
- [ ] **envious** 形 うらやんで
- [ ] **envision** 動 想像する，思いめぐらす
- [ ] **envy** 名 うらやましさ，嫉妬，羨望 動 うらやましがる，嫉妬する
- [ ] **equally** 副 等しく，平等に

142

□ **equip** 動備え付ける, 装備する

□ **Eric Hoffer** エリック・ホッファー《アメリカの社会哲学者, 1902–1983》

□ **err** 動間違う, 過ちを犯す

□ **error** 名誤り, 間違い, 過失

□ **escape** 動逃げる, 免れる, もれる 名逃亡, 脱出, もれ

□ **essay** 名エッセイ, 随筆

□ **essayist** 名エッセイスト, 随筆家

□ **essence** 名①本質, 真髄, 最重要点 ②エッセンス, エキス

□ **eternity** 名永遠, 永久

□ **evasion** 名①〔義務などを〕逃れること, 回避すること ②言い逃れ

□ **eve** 名前日, 前夜

□ **even if** たとえ～でも

□ **eventually** 副結局は

□ **ever** 熟 **if ever** もし～ということがあれば

□ **every day** 毎日

□ **every time** ～するときはいつも

□ **everybody** 代誰でも, 皆

□ **everyday** 形毎日の, 日々の

□ **everyone** 代誰でも, 皆

□ **everything** 代すべてのこと[もの], 何でも, 何もかも

□ **everywhere** 副どこにいても, いたるところに

□ **evil** 形①邪悪な ②有害な, 不吉な 名①邪悪 ②害, わざわい, 不幸 副悪く

□ **examination** 名試験, 審査, 検査, 診察

□ **example** 熟 **for example** たとえば

□ **except** 前～を除いて, ～のほかは 接～ということを除いて

□ **exception** 名例外, 除外, 異論

□ **excessive** 形度を超えた, 行き過ぎた, 極端な

□ **exercise** 名①運動, 体操 ②練習 動①運動する, 練習する ②影響を及ぼす

□ **exert** 動①(力・知力・能力を)出す, 発揮する ②(権力を)行使する

□ **exist** 動存在する, 生存する, ある, いる

□ **existence** 名存在, 実在, 生存

□ **expand** 動①広げる, 拡張[拡大]する ②発展させる, 拡充する

□ **expect** 動予期[予測]する, (当然のこととして)期待する

□ **expectation** 名期待, 予期, 可能性, 見込み

□ **explanation** 名①説明, 解説, 釈明 ②解釈, 意味

□ **expose** 動①さらす, 露出する ②(秘密などを)暴露する ③商品を陳列する

□ **express** 動表現する, 述べる 形①明白な ②急行の 名速達便, 急行列車 副速達で, 急行で

□ **extensively** 副幅広く, 広範囲に(わたって)

□ **extra** 形余分の, 臨時の 名①余分なもの ②エキストラ 副余分に

□ **extract** 動抜粋する, 抽出する 名抽出したもの

F

□ **fact** 熟 **in fact** つまり, 実は, 要するに

□ **faculty** 名①(大学の)学部 ②能力 ③(身体・精神の)機能

□ **fail** 動①失敗する, 落第する[させる] ②《 – to ～》～し損なう, ～できない ③失望させる 名失敗, 落第点

□ **failure** 名①失敗, 落第 ②不足, 欠乏 ③停止, 減退

□ **faint** 形かすかな, 弱い, ぼんやりした 動気絶する 名気絶, 失神

□ **fair** 形①正しい, 公平[正当]な ②

快晴の ③色白の, 金髪の ④かなりの ⑤《古》美しい 副①公平に, きれいに ②見事に

□ **fairy** 名妖精 形妖精の(ような)

□ **fairyland** 名①〔架空の〕おとぎ[妖精]の国 ②〔空想の〕理想郷

□ **faith** 名①信念, 信仰 ②信頼, 信用

□ **faithful** 形忠実な, 正確な

□ **faithless** 形不誠実な, 信念のない

□ **fall down** 落ちる, ひっくり返る

□ **fallen** 動fall (落ちる)の過去分詞 形落ちた, 倒れた

□ **familiarity** 名熟知, 親しさ, なれなれしさ **familiarity with** ～に熟知していること

□ **fanciful** 形空想の, 想像上の

□ **fancy** 名①幻想, 空想 ②想像力 形①装飾的な, 見事な ②法外な, 高級な 動①心に描く, (～と)考える ②好む, 引かれる

□ **far** 熟**as far as** ～まで, ～する限り(では) **by far** はるかに, 断然 **far from** ～から遠い **far too** あまりにも～過ぎる

□ **farce** 名①笑劇, 茶番劇 ②〔状況や出来事の〕茶番, 笑いぐさ

□ **fatal** 形致命的な, 運命を決する

□ **fate** 名①《時にF-》運命, 宿命 ②破滅, 悲運 動(～の)運命にある

□ **fault** 名①欠点, 短所 ②過失, 誤り 動とがめる

□ **favor** 熟**in favor of** ～を支持して, ～を好んで

□ **favorable** 形好意的な, 都合のよい

□ **fear** 名①恐れ ②心配, 不安 動①恐れる ②心配する

□ **feature** 名①特徴, 特色 ②顔の一部,《-s》顔立ち ③(ラジオ・テレビ・新聞などの)特集 動①(～の)特徴になる ②呼び物にする

□ **feed** 動①食物を与える ②供給する 名①飼育, 食事 ②供給

□ **feel like** ～したい気がする, ～のような感じがする

□ **feeling** 動feel (感じる)の現在分詞 名①感じ, 気持ち ②触感, 知覚 ③同情, 思いやり, 感受性 形感じる, 感じやすい, 情け深い

□ **fellah** 名①男, 男の子, やつ ②仲間, 同志(= fellow)

□ **fellow-creature** 名同胞, 身近な仲間

□ **female** 形女性の, 婦人の, 雌の 名婦人, 雌

□ **fender** 名①衝撃から守るためのもの[装置] ②〈米〉〔自動車の〕泥よけ

□ **fiber** 名①繊維, 食物繊維, 繊維質 ②性格, 性質 ③強さ, 堅牢性

□ **fickle** 形①〔天候などが〕変わりやすい ②〔人が好みの対象をコロコロ変えて〕気まぐれな, 移り気な

□ **fiction** 名フィクション, 作り話, 小説

□ **fierce** 形どう猛な, 荒々しい, すさまじい, 猛烈な

□ **fiercely** 副どう猛に, 猛烈に

□ **fight with** ～と戦う

□ **fighting** 名闘い, 戦闘

□ **filled with** 《be –》～でいっぱいになる

□ **final** 形最後の, 決定的な

□ **finishing** 動finish (終わる)の現在分詞 形仕上げの, 最後の 名仕上げ

□ **first** 熟**for the first time** 初めて

□ **fit** 形①適当な, 相応な ②体の調子がよい 動合致[適合]する, 合致させる

□ **flavor** 名風味, 味わい, 趣 動風味を添える

□ **flesh** 名肉,《the –》肉体

□ **flight** 名飛ぶこと, 飛行, (飛行機の)フライト

□ **flinch** 動①〔恐れや痛みに思わず〕

後ろへ下がる，ぎくりとする ②〔困難・不快なことなどに〕たじろぐ，尻込みする

□ **float** 動浮かぶ，浮く

□ **flurried** 形混乱した，気が転倒した

□ **flushed** 形〔顔が〕赤くなった，紅潮した

□ **flying** 動fly（飛ぶ）の現在分詞 名飛行 形飛んでいる，空中に浮かぶ，（飛ぶように）速い

□ **focus** 名①焦点，ピント ②関心の的，着眼点 ③中心 動①焦点を合わせる ②（関心・注意を）集中させる

□ **foe** 名敵，（競争の）相手

□ **fold** 名折り目，ひだ 動①折りたたむ，包む ②（手を）組む

□ **following** 動follow（ついていく）の現在分詞 形《the –》次の，次に続く 名《the –》下記のもの，以下に述べるもの

□ **folly** 名愚行，おろかさ

□ **fool** 名①ばか者，おろかな人 ②道化師 動ばかにする，だます，ふざける

□ **foolish** 形おろかな，ばかばかしい

□ **for** 熟It is ~ for someone to …（人）が~するのは~だ **as for** ~に関しては，~はどうかと言うと **call for** ~を求める，~を呼び求める，呼び出す **care for** ~の世話をする，~を気遣う，~を大事に思う **for example** たとえば **for oneself** 独力で，自分のために **for some reason** なんらかの理由で，どういうわけか **for the first time** 初めて **for ~ years** ~年間，~年にわたって **make a stand for** ~を擁護する，~を支持する **pass for** ~として通用する **reason for** ~の理由

□ **force** 名力，勢い 動①強制する，力ずくで~する，余儀なく~させる ②押しやる，押し込む

□ **foregone** 形過去の，既定の

□ **forgetful** 形忘れっぽい，無頓着な

□ **forgive** 動許す，免除する

□ **forgiveness** 名許す（こと），寛容

□ **form** 名①形，形式 ②書式 動形づくる

□ **former** 形①前の，先の，以前の ②《the –》（二者のうち）前者の

□ **forsake** 動~を見捨てる，~を見放す

□ **fortitude** 名不屈の精神，忍耐力

□ **fortunate** 形幸運な，幸運をもたらす

□ **fortune** 名①富，財産 ②幸運，繁栄，チャンス ③運命，運勢

□ **forward** 形①前方の，前方へ向かう ②将来の ③先の 副①前方に ②将来に向けて ③先へ，進んで

□ **foster** 動①育てる，促進させる ②心に抱く 形里親の

□ **foul** 形悪臭のある，不潔な，汚い，ひどい

□ **foundation** 名①建設，創設 ②基礎，土台

□ **four-footer** 名四つ足の動物

□ **fox** 名キツネ（狐）

□ **fragrance** 名芳香

□ **fragrant** 形香りのよい

□ **frail** 形もろい，はかない，弱い

□ **frame** 名骨組み，構造，額縁 動形づくる，組み立てる

□ **Francis Bacon** フランシス・ベーコン《イギリスの哲学者・政治家，1561–1626》

□ **frank** 形率直な，隠し立てをしない

□ **frankness** 名〔意見などの〕率直さ

□ **freely** 副自由に，障害なしに

□ **frequently** 副頻繁に，しばしば

□ **freshly** 副新しく，~したてで，新鮮に，はつらつと

□ **Friedrich Nietzsche** フリードリヒ・ニーチェ《ドイツの哲学者・古典文献学者，1844–1900》

□ **friendship** 名友人であること，友

情

□ **frighten** 動驚かせる, びっくりさせる

□ **frivolous** 形くだらない, 軽薄な

□ **from** 熟far from ～から遠い from ～ to … ～から…まで

□ **front** 熟in front of ～の前に, ～の正面に

□ **frost** 名霜, 寒気

□ **fruitless** 形成果のない, 実を結ばない, 不毛の

□ **frying pan** フライパン

□ **fulfill** 動（義務・約束を）果たす, (要求・条件を)満たす

□ **full-blown** 形①〔花が〕満開の, 十分に開花した ②成熟した, 十分に発育〔発達〕した ③万全の, 本格的な

□ **fun** 熟have fun 楽しむ

□ **funeral** 名葬式, 葬列 形葬式の

□ **funnel** 動①じょうで～に注ぐ ②(資金などを)つぎ込む 名じょうご(形のもの)

□ **further** 形いっそう遠い, その上の, なおいっそうの 副いっそう遠く, その上に, もっと 動促進する

□ **fury** 名激しさ, 激怒, 激情

□ **fusible** 形溶けやすい, 可溶性の

G

□ **gable** 名《建築》切妻, 破風

□ **gain** 動①得る, 増す ②進歩する, 進む 名①増加, 進歩 ②利益, 得ること, 獲得

□ **gather** 動①集まる, 集める ②生じる, 増す ③推測する

□ **gathering** 動gather（集まる）の現在分詞 名①集まり, 集会 ②ひだ, ギャザー

□ **general** 形①全体の, 一般の, 普通の ②おおよその ③（職位の）高い, 上級の in general 一般に, たいてい

□ 名大将, 将軍

□ **generally** 副①一般に, だいたい ②たいてい

□ **generous** 形①寛大な, 気前のよい ②豊富な

□ **gentle** 形①優しい, 温和な ②柔らかな

□ **George** 名ジョージ《人名》

□ **get into** 〔習慣や癖などを〕身に付ける

□ **get on** 時が経つ, 先に進む

□ **get to do** ～できるようになる

□ **ghost** 名幽霊

□ **gift** 名①贈り物 ②(天賦の)才能 動授ける

□ **glamour** 名魅力

□ **glimpse** 名ちらりと見ること 動ちらりと見る

□ **glitter** 動①きらきら輝く, きらめく ②派手である 名輝き, 華麗さ

□ **globe** 名①球 ②地球

□ **gloomy** 形①憂うつな, 陰気な ②うす暗い

□ **glorious** 形①栄誉に満ちた, 輝かしい ②荘厳な, すばらしい

□ **gloriously** 副①光り輝いて ②〔光り輝くかのごとく〕素晴らしく, 見事に

□ **glow** 動①(火が)白熱して輝く ②(体が)ほてる 名①白熱, 輝き ②ほてり, 熱情

□ **go away** 立ち去る

□ **go doing** ～をしに行く

□ **go on** 続く, 進み続ける, 起こる

□ **go out of** ～から出る〔消える〕

□ **go to sleep** 寝る

□ **golden** 形①金色の ②金製の ③貴重な

□ **good** 熟as good as ～も同然で, ほとんど～

□ **gooseflesh** 名〔寒さ・恐怖などに

よって皮膚に生じる〕鳥肌

- □ **govern** 動治める, 管理する, 支配する
- □ **grass** 图草, 牧草(地), 芝生 動草[芝生]で覆う[覆われる]
- □ **grave** 图墓 形重要な, 厳粛な, 落ち着いた
- □ **gravestone** 图墓石
- □ **greed** 图どん欲, 欲張り
- □ **green-eyed** 形①緑色の目をした ②嫉妬深い
- □ **grey** 形①灰色の ②どんよりした, 憂うつな ③白髪の 图灰色
- □ **grief** 图(深い)悲しみ, 悲嘆
- □ **grip** 動しっかりつかむ 图①つかむこと, 把握, グリップ ②支配(力)
- □ **growing-up** 图成長(すること)
- □ **guarantee** 图保証, 保証書, 保証人 動保証する, 請け合う
- □ **guard** 图①警戒, 見張り ②番人 動番をする, 監視する, 守る
- □ **guardian** 图保護者, 守護神
- □ **guest** 图客, ゲスト
- □ **guilt** 图罪, 有罪, 犯罪
- □ **guilty** 形有罪の, やましい

H

- □ **habit** 图習慣, 癖, 気質
- □ **hall** 图公会堂, ホール, 大広間, 玄関
- □ **hand** 熟on the other hand 一方, 他方では
- □ **hang** 動かかる, かける, つるす, ぶら下がる 图①かかり具合 ②《the -》扱い方, こつ
- □ **happen to** ～に起こる, たまたま～する
- □ **happiness** 图幸せ, 喜び
- □ **hard to** ～し難い
- □ **hardly** 副①ほとんど～でない, わ

ずかに ②厳しく, かろうじて

- □ **Harry** 图ハリー《人名》
- □ **haste** 图急ぐこと, あわてること **in haste** 急いで
- □ **hasty** 形①急ぎの, あわただしい ②早まった, 軽率な
- □ **hath** 動have(持つ)の直説法3人称単数・現在形(=has)
- □ **hatred** 图憎しみ, 毛嫌い
- □ **haunt** 動よく行く, 出没する, つきまとう
- □ **have** 熟could have done ～だったかもしれない《仮定法》 have fun 楽しむ have no choice but to ～ するしかない have nothing to do with ～と何の関係もない
- □ **heal** 動いえる, いやす, 治る, 治す
- □ **healthy** 形健康な, 健全な, 健康によい
- □ **heart** 熟by heart 暗記して
- □ **heart-ease** 图心の平和
- □ **heartache** 图心痛, 苦悩, 悲嘆
- □ **heaven** 图①天国 ②天国のようなところ[状態], 楽園 ③空 ④《H-》神
- □ **height** 图①高さ, 身長 ②《the -》絶頂, 真っ盛り ③高台, 丘
- □ **Helen Rowland** ヘレン・ローランド《アメリカのジャーナリストでウィットに富んだコラムを得意とした, 1875-1950》
- □ **hell** 图地獄, 地獄のようなところ[状態]
- □ **helpful** 形役に立つ, 参考になる
- □ **hence** 副①だから, それ故に ②今から, 今後
- □ **heritage** 图遺産, 相続財産
- □ **highly** 副①大いに, 非常に ②高度に, 高位に ③高く評価して, 高価で
- □ **hindsight** 图あとになっての判断, 後知恵
- □ **hollow** 图①へこみ ②空白 形うつろな, くぼんだ

□ **home** 熟 at home 自宅で, 在宅して

□ **homesick** 形 家を恋しがる, 故郷を慕う, ホームシックの

□ **honesty** 名 正直, 誠実

□ **how often** どのくらいの頻度で, 何回〜ですか

□ **how to** 〜する方法

□ **however** 副 たとえ〜でも 接 けれども, だが

□ **huge** 形 巨大な, ばく大な

□ **human being** 人間

□ **humanity** 名 人間性, 人間らしさ

□ **humble** 形 つつましい, 粗末な 動 卑しめる, 謙虚にさせる

□ **humility** 名 謙遜, 謙虚, 卑下

□ **humorist** 名 ①ユーモアのある[を解する]人 ②ユーモア作家[俳優]

□ **humour** 名 ①ユーモア ②(一時的な)機嫌 動 機嫌をとる

□ **hunger** 名 ①空腹, 飢え ②(〜への)欲 動 ①飢える ②熱望する

□ **hunting** 動 hunt (狩る)の現在分詞 名 狩り, 狩猟, ハンティング, 捜索 形 狩猟の

□ **hurricane** 名 ハリケーン

I

□ **I wish 〜 were ...** 私が〜なら…なのに。《仮定法過去》

□ **i.e.** すなわち, 言い換えれば《ラテン語 id est の略》

□ **ideal** 名 理想, 究極の目標 形 理想的な, 申し分のない

□ **identity** 名 ①同一であること ②本人であること ③独自性

□ **idiom** 名 慣用句, 熟語, 成句

□ **idyllic** 形 のどかな, 牧歌的な, 素晴らしい

□ **if** 熟 If + 《主語》+ could 〜 できればなあ《仮定法》as if あたかも〜のように, まるで〜みたいに **even if** たとえ〜でも **if ever** もし〜ということがあれば

□ **ignorance** 名 無知, 無学

□ **ignorant** 形 ①無知な, 無学な ②知らないで, 気づかないで

□ **ignore** 動 無視する, 怠る

□ **illuminate** 動 ①照らす, 明るくする ②イルミネーションを施す ③啓蒙する

□ **illusion** 名 ①錯覚, 幻想 ②勘違い, 見間違い

□ **image** 名 ①印象, 姿 ②画像, 映像 動 心に描く, 想像する

□ **imagination** 名 想像(力), 空想

□ **imagine** 動 想像する, 心に思い描く

□ **imbedded** 形 ①〔物が表面下に〕埋め込まれた, はめ込まれた ②〔感情などが〕深く［強く］根付いた (= embedded)

□ **imitation** 名 ①模倣, まね ②模造品

□ **immature** 形 ①未熟な ②〈非難を表して〉〔人の言動や考え方が〕子どもっぽい, 大人げない 名 未熟者

□ **immaturity** 名 未熟

□ **immeasurable** 形 計り知れない(ほどの)

□ **immemorial** 形 大昔の, 太古の

□ **immense** 形 巨大な, 計り知れない, すばらしい

□ **immortal** 形 ①死ぬことのない, 不死の ②不滅の 名 不死の人

□ **immunity** 名 免疫, 免除

□ **imperative** 形 ①必要不可欠の, 必須の ②〈文〉高圧的な, 威圧的な ③避け［逃れ］られない

□ **imply** 動 暗示する, ほのめかす, 暗に含む

□ **importance** 名 重要性, 大切さ

□ **improve** 動 改善する［させる］, 進

歩する

- □ **in accordance with** ～に従って
- □ **in fact** つまり, 実は, 要するに
- □ **in favor of** ～を支持して, ～を好んで
- □ **in front of** ～の前に, ～の正面に
- □ **in general** 一般に, たいてい
- □ **in haste** 急いで
- □ **in order to** ～するために, ～しようと
- □ **in other words** すなわち, 言い換えれば
- □ **in public** 人前で, 公然と
- □ **in short** 要約すると
- □ **in the direction of** ～の方向に
- □ **in the end** とうとう, 結局, ついに
- □ **in the same way as [that]** ～ ～と同じように
- □ **in the world** 世界で
- □ **in time** 間に合って, やがて
- □ **in vain** むだに, むなしく
- □ **inanimate** 形①生きていない, 生命のない, 無生物の ②〔動作・表情などが〕生気のない, 活気のない
- □ **incident** 名出来事, 事故, 事変, 紛争 形①起こりがちな ②付随する
- □ **incidentally** 副偶然に
- □ **include** 動含む, 勘定に入れる
- □ **incongruous** 形①〔二つの要素・物事などが〕調和〔釣り合い〕のとれていない, ちぐはぐの ②〔話などが〕つじつまの合わない ③〔道理などに〕適わない
- □ **inconsequential** 形重要ではない, 取るに足りない
- □ **inconsistent** 形一貫していない, 矛盾した
- □ **incorrect** 形正しくない, 間違った
- □ **indeed** 副①実際, 本当に ②《強意》まったく 間本当に, まさか
- □ **independent** 形独立した, 自立

した

- □ **independently** 副独立して, 自主的に, 独力で
- □ **indescribable** 形言葉で言い表せない, 筆舌に尽くしがたい
- □ **indicate** 動①指す, 示す, 〔道などを〕教える ②それとなく言う ③きざしがある
- □ **indirect** 形間接的な, 二次的な
- □ **indiscretion** 名①無分別, 軽率さ ②無分別〔軽率〕な言動
- □ **individual** 形独立した, 個性的な, 個々の 名個体, 個人
- □ **infinitely** 副無限に
- □ **infinitesimal** 形微小な〔の〕, 非常に小さな〔小さい〕
- □ **influence** 名影響, 勢力 動影響をおよぼす
- □ **infuse** 動①〔強い感情や熱意を〕注ぐ, 注入する ②〔人に考えなどを〕吹き込む, 〔人の心をある感情で〕満たす
- □ **ingenuity** 名発明の才, 巧妙さ, 独創性
- □ **inject** 動注射〔注入〕する
- □ **injection** 名①注入, 注射 ②(資金の)つぎ込み, 投入
- □ **injustice** 名不当, 不正(行為)
- □ **inmost** 形①最も奥の ②心の奥の, 深く心に秘めた
- □ **inner** 形①内部の ②心の中の
- □ **innocence** 名①無邪気, 純真 ②無罪, 潔白
- □ **innocent** 名無邪気な人, 罪のない人 形無邪気な, 無実の
- □ **inordinate** 形①過度の, 法外な, 並外れた ②〈文〉無秩序な, 混乱した
- □ **insect** 名虫, 昆虫
- □ **insight** 名洞察, 真相, 見識
- □ **inspiring** 形鼓舞する, 感激させる
- □ **instant** 形即時の, 緊急の, 即席の 名瞬間, 寸時

- [ ] **instead** 副その代わりに **instead of**～の代わりに、～をしないで
- [ ] **instill** 動吹き込む、教え込む
- [ ] **instinct** 名①本能、天性 ②直感
- [ ] **institution** 名①設立、制定 ②制度、慣習 ③協会、公共団体
- [ ] **instruction** 名教えること、指示、助言
- [ ] **insufficient** 形①不十分な、不足して ②不適当な、能力のない
- [ ] **insult** 動侮辱する、ばかにする 名侮辱、無礼な言動
- [ ] **intellectual** 形知的な、知性のある 名知識人、有識者
- [ ] **intelligence** 名①知能 ②情報
- [ ] **intelligent** 形頭のよい、聡明な
- [ ] **intense** 形①強烈な、激しい ②感情的な
- [ ] **intentional** 形故意の、意図的な
- [ ] **interchangeable** 形互いに交換[代替]できる、置き換え可能な
- [ ] **interesting** 動interest（興味を起こさせる）の現在分詞 形おもしろい、興味を起こさせる
- [ ] **interval** 名間隔、距離、合間
- [ ] **intimacy** 名親密さ、親しい関係
- [ ] **into** 熟**break into pieces** 粉々になる、砕け散る **carry into** ～の中に運び入れる、持ち込む **come into** ～に入ってくる **get into**〔習慣や癖などを〕身に付ける **put ～ into words** ～をを言葉で表す[表現する]、～を言葉にする **turn into** ～に変わる
- [ ] **intriguing** 形興味をそそる、魅力的な
- [ ] **invent** 動①発明[考案]する ②ねつ造する
- [ ] **investment** 名投資、出資
- [ ] **invisible** 名目に見えないもの 形目に見えない、表に出ない
- [ ] **Ireland** 名アイルランド《国名》
- [ ] **irony** 名皮肉、反語、あてこすり

- [ ] **irritate** 動いらいらさせる、怒らせる
- [ ] **It is ～ for someone to ...**（人）が…するのは～だ
- [ ] **It is ～ of A to ...** Aが…するのは～だ
- [ ] **item** 名①項目、品目 ②（新聞など の）記事
- [ ] **itself** 代それ自体、それ自身

J

- [ ] **J. L. Carr** J・L・カー《イギリスの小説家。本名はジョセフ・ロイド・カー（Joseph Lloyd Carr）、1912–1994》
- [ ] **Japanese** 形日本（人・語）の 名①日本人 ②日本語
- [ ] **jealous** 形嫉妬して、嫉妬深い、うらやんで
- [ ] **jealousy** 名嫉妬、ねたみ
- [ ] **Jean Sibelius** ジャン・シベリウス《フィンランドの作曲家・ヴァイオリニスト、1865–1957》
- [ ] **Jo Nesbo** ジョー・ネスボ《ノルウェーの小説家・ミュージシャン、1960–》
- [ ] **John F. Kennedy** ジョン・F・ケネディ《任期1961～1963年の第35代アメリカ合衆国大統領、1917–1963》
- [ ] **Jolyon** 名ジョリオン《人名》
- [ ] **journalist** 名報道関係者、ジャーナリスト
- [ ] **journey** 名①（遠い目的地への）旅 ②行程
- [ ] **joy** 名喜び、楽しみ
- [ ] **joyful** 形楽しませる、喜びに満ちた
- [ ] **judge** 動判決を下す、裁く、判断する、評価する 名裁判官、判事、審査員
- [ ] **judicious** 形思慮分別のある、賢明な
- [ ] **just as**（ちょうど）であろうとおり
- [ ] **justice** 名①公平、公正、正当、正義

②司法, 裁判(官)

K

- □ **kernel** 名 ①《植物》外皮の中の実 [種子] ②〈比喩〉中心部 ③〈比喩〉[問題などの]核心, 要点
- □ **kind of** ある程度, いくらか, ～のようなもの[人]
- □ **know of** ～について知っている
- □ **knowledge** 名 知識, 理解, 学問

L

- □ **lack** 動 不足している, 欠けている 名 不足, 欠乏
- □ **lamentation** 名 悲嘆, 哀悼
- □ **lamp** 名 ランプ, 灯火
- □ **landscape** 名 ①景色, 風景 ②見晴らし ③風景画
- □ **lap** 動《波が～に》打ち寄せる
- □ **large** 名 a large number of 大量の～, 多くの～
- □ **lark** 名 ①ヒバリ《雲雀》《鳥》 ②浮かれ, たわむれ, 冗談 動 たわむれる, ふざける
- □ **last** 熟 at last ついに, とうとう
- □ **lasting** 動 last《続く》の現在分詞 形 長持ちする, 永続する
- □ **Latin** 名 ①ラテン語 ②ラテン系民族の人 形 ラテン(語・系)の
- □ **latter** 形 ①後の, 末の, 後者の ②《the –》後者《代名詞的に用いる》
- □ **laugh at** ～を見て[聞いて]笑う
- □ **laughter** 名 笑い(声)
- □ **lay** 動 ①置く, 横たえる, 敷く ②整える ③卵を産む ④lie《横たわる》の過去
- □ **laziness** 名 怠惰
- □ **lead to** ～に至る, ～を引き起こす

- □ **leadeth** 動 lead《導く》の3人称単数・現在形(= leads)
- □ **league** 名 ①同盟, 連盟 ②《スポーツの》競技連盟
- □ **lean** 動 ①もたれる, 寄りかかる ②傾く, 傾ける 形 やせた, 不毛の
- □ **least** 形 いちばん小さい, 最も少ない 副 いちばん小さく, 最も少なく 名 最小, 最少 at least 少なくとも
- □ **leather** 名 皮革, 皮製品
- □ **leave behind** あとにする, ～を置き去りにする
- □ **leeway** 名 〈話〉[時間・金などの]余裕, ゆとり
- □ **leisure** 名 余暇 at leisure ゆっくり, 暇で 形 余暇の
- □ **lend** 動 貸す, 貸し出す
- □ **Leopold Stokowski** レオポルド・ストコフスキー《イギリス生まれの指揮者で「音の魔術師」の異名を持つ, 1882–1977》
- □ **less** 形 ～より小さい[少ない] 副 ～より少なく, ～ほどでなく
- □ **lessen** 動 《物, 事を》少なく[小さく]する, 減らす
- □ **let us** どうか私たちに～させてください
- □ **level** 名 ①水平, 平面 ②水準 形 ①水平の, 平たい ②同等[同位]の 動 ①水平にする ②平等にする
- □ **liar** 名 うそつき
- □ **liberator** 名 解放者
- □ **liberty** 名 ①自由, 解放 ②《-ties》特権, 特典 ③《-ties》勝手な振る舞い
- □ **lie** 動 ①うそをつく ②横たわる, 寝る ③《ある状態に》ある, 存在する 名 うそ, 詐欺
- □ **life** 熟 come to life 目覚める, 復活する
- □ **life-blood** 名 生き血
- □ **lightning** 名 電光, 雷, 稲妻
- □ **like** 熟 feel like ～したい気がす

A B C D E F G H I J K L M N O P Q R S T U V W X Y Z

る，〜のような感じがする **look like** 〜のように見える，〜に似ている **would like to** 〜したいと思う

- **likely** 形 ①ありそうな，(〜)しそうな ②適当な 副 たぶん，おそらく
- **limb** 名 ①手足，四肢 ②大枝
- **limit** 名 限界，《-s》範囲，境界 動 制限［限定］する
- **limitation** 名 制限，限度
- **limited** 動 limit（制限する）の過去，過去分詞 形 限られた，限定の
- **link** 名 ①(鎖の)輪 ②リンク ③相互［因果］関係 動 連結する，つながる
- **lip** 名 唇，《-s》口
- **list** 名 名簿，目録，一覧表 動 名簿［目録］に記入する
- **listener** 名 聞く人，ラジオ聴取者
- **literature** 名 文学，文芸
- **live up to** 〔主義・信念など〕に従って行動［生活］する
- **liver** 名 肝臓
- **living** 動 live（住む）の現在分詞 名 生計，生活 形 ①生きている，現存の ②使用されている ③そっくりの
- **loathe** 動 大嫌いである，ひどく嫌う
- **Logan Pearsall Smith** ローガン・ピアソル・スミス《アメリカのエッセイスト・批評家，1865–1946》
- **loiter** 動 うろつく，道草を食う
- **loneliness** 名 孤独
- **lonely** 形 ①孤独な，心さびしい ②ひっそりした，人里離れた
- **lonesome** 形 さびしい，人気のない
- **long** 熟 **as long as** 〜する以上は，〜である限りは **no longer** もはや〜でない［〜しない］ **so long as** 〜する限りは
- **look** 熟 **look like** 〜のように見える，〜に似ている **look upon** 〜を見る，見つめる **take a look at** 〜をち

ょっと見る

- **loose** 形 自由な，ゆるんだ，あいまいな 動 ほどく，解き放つ
- **lord** 名 首長，主人，領主，貴族，上院議員
- **lose sight of** 〜を見失う
- **loss** 名 ①損失(額・物)，損害，浪費 ②失敗，敗北
- **lot** 熟 **a lot of** たくさんの〜
- **lottery** 名 宝くじ，くじ引き
- **lovable** 形 愛すべき，かわいい
- **lovely** 形 愛らしい，美しい，すばらしい
- **lover** 名 ①愛人，恋人 ②愛好者
- **loving** 動 love（愛する）の現在分詞 形 愛する，愛情のこもった
- **loyal** 形 忠実な，誠実な 名 忠実，愛国者
- **lubricate** 動 ①〜に潤滑油［剤］を塗る［差す］ ②〔物事を〕円滑に動かす［運営する］
- **luck** 熟 **bad luck** 災難，不運
- **lukewarm** 形 なまぬるい
- **luxury** 形 豪華な，高級な，贅沢な 名 豪華さ，贅沢(品)
- **lying** 動 lie（うそをつく・横たわる）の現在分詞 形 ①うそをつく，虚偽の ②横になっている 名 ①うそをつくこと，虚言，虚偽 ②横たわること

M

- **machinery** 名 機械類［装置］
- **Macumazahn** 名 マクマザーン《人名》
- **mad** 形 ①気の狂った ②逆上した，理性をなくした ③ばかげた ④(〜に)熱狂［熱中］して，夢中の
- **madding** 形 狂気の，狂乱の
- **made out of** 《be –》〜で作られている

- **mademoiselle** 名〈フランス語〉マドモアゼル, お嬢さま《敬称または呼び掛けに用いられる》
- **madman** 名①狂人 ②常軌を逸した人
- **magic** 名①魔法, 手品 ②魔力 形魔法の, 魔力のある
- **magnificent** 形壮大な, 壮麗な, すばらしい
- **main** 形主な, 主要な
- **make a stand for** 〜を擁護する, 〜を支持する
- **making** 動make (作る) の現在分詞 名制作, 製造
- **malevolent** 形悪意のある, 邪悪な, 害悪を及ぼす
- **malleable** 形①〔人が他人に〕影響されやすい ②〔人が〕従順な
- **manage** 動①動かす, うまく処理する ②経営 [管理]する, 支配する ③どうにか〜する
- **manhood** 名大人の男, 成年, 男らしさ
- **mankind** 名人類, 人間
- **manner** 名①方法, やり方 ②態度, 様子 ③《-s》行儀, 作法, 生活様式
- **many** 熟many a いくつもの〜, 数々の〜　so many 非常に多くの
- **marble** 名①大理石, 大理石模様 ②ビー玉 動大理石模様をつける
- **mark** 名①印, 記号, 跡 ②点数 ③特色 動①印 [記号]をつける ②採点する ③目立たせる
- **marriage** 名①結婚(生活・式) ②結合, 融合, (吸収)合併
- **married** 動marry (結婚する) の過去, 過去分詞 形結婚した, 既婚の
- **marry** 動結婚する
- **marvellous** 形驚くべき, 驚嘆すべき, すばらしい
- **master** 名主人, 雇い主, 師, 名匠 動①修得する ②〜の主となる
- **mate** 名仲間, 連れ 動①交尾する [させる] ②仲間になる, 結婚する
- **matrimony** 名①結婚していること, 結婚生活 ②結婚すること, 結婚式
- **meaning** 名①意味, 趣旨 ②重要性
- **means** 熟by no means 決して〜ではない
- **measureless** 形計り知れない(ほどの)
- **mechanism** 名機構, 仕組み
- **medical** 形①医学の ②内科の 名健康診断, 身体検査
- **mediocrity** 名①〔質や能力などが〕凡庸 [月並み]なこと ②凡庸 [月並み]な能力 [成果], 凡才
- **melancholy** 形もの悲しい, 憂うつな, ふさぎ込んだ 名哀愁, 憂うつ, うつ病
- **memory** 名記憶(力), 思い出
- **mention** 動(〜について)述べる, 言及する 名言及, 陳述
- **merchant** 名商人, 貿易商
- **merciful** 形慈悲深い
- **mercy** 名①情け, 哀れみ, 慈悲 ②ありがたいこと, 幸運
- **mere** 形単なる, ほんの, まったく 〜にすぎない
- **merely** 副単に, たかが〜に過ぎない
- **merited** 形〔称賛・尊敬などを得ることが〕当然の
- **mermaid** 名(女の)人魚
- **metaphor** 名①《言語学》隠喩, 暗喩, メタファー ②〔隠喩の〕例え, 象徴
- **metropolitan** 形首都の, 大都会の
- **Michael Levine** マイケル・レヴィン《アメリカの作曲家・脚本家, 1964-》

□ **middle** 名中間, 最中 形中間の, 中央の

□ **midnight-blue** 名ミッドナイトブルー《色の一つで, ごく暗い紫みの青》

□ **might** 助《mayの過去》①〜かもしれない ②〜してもよい, 〜できる 名力, 権力

□ **mill** 名①製造所 ②ミル, ひき機 動ひく

□ **mind** 名①心, 精神, 考え ②知性 動①気にする, いやがる ②気をつける, 用心する

□ **mingle** 動入り混じる, 混ざる

□ **minister** 名①大臣, 閣僚, 公使 ②聖職者

□ **miracle** 名奇跡(的な出来事), 不思議なこと

□ **mirth** 名陽気, 歓楽, 浮かれ騒ぎ

□ **mischief** 名いたずら, (損)害

□ **mischievous** 形いたずらな

□ **miserable** 形みじめな, 哀れな

□ **misery** 名①悲惨, みじめさ ②苦痛, 不幸, 苦難

□ **misfortune** 名不運, 不幸, 災難

□ **mislay** 動〜を間違った場所に置く

□ **misleading** 動mislead (間違った方向へ導く)の現在分詞 形人を誤らせる, 誤解を招くような

□ **mist** 名①霧, もや, 蒸気 ②(目の)かすみ 動①霧がかかる, 霧で覆う ②(目が)かすむ

□ **mitigate** 動〔怒り・苦痛などを〕和らげる

□ **mocking** 形嘲る(ような)

□ **moderate** 形穏やかな, 適度な, 手ごろな 動穏やかにする, 抑える

□ **moderation** 名節度, 控えめ, 中庸

□ **modern** 形現代[近代]の, 現代的な, 最近の 名現代[近代]人

□ **modest** 形控えめな, 謙虚な

□ **mole** 名①モグラ ②ほくろ, あざ

□ **moment** 名①瞬間, ちょっとの間 ②(特定の)時, 時期

□ **monseigneur** 名〈フランス語〉閣下, 僧正

□ **monster** 名怪物

□ **mood** 名気分, 機嫌, 雰囲気, 憂うつ

□ **moonstone** 名《鉱物》ムーンストーン, 月長石

□ **moral** 形道徳(上)の, 倫理的な, 道徳的な 名教訓, 品行, モラル

□ **moralist** 名モラリスト, 倫理学者

□ **more** 名more than 〜以上 no more 〜 than… …ほど〜なものはない the more 〜 the more … 〜すればするほどますます…

□ **Morley** 名モーリー《人名》

□ **mortal** 形①死ぬ運命にある ②人間の ③致命的な 名①死すべきもの ②人間

□ **mosquito** 名カ(蚊)

□ **motif** 名〔文学作品の〕主題, モチーフ《作品中に繰り返し現れるその作品のテーマとなるもの》

□ **motive** 名動機, 目的, モチーフ

□ **mournful** 形悲しい, 哀れを誘う, 陰気な

□ **mourning** 名①悲嘆, 哀悼 ②服喪, 哀悼の意を表すこと

□ **mouse** 名(ハツカ)ネズミ

□ **much** 熟as much as 〜と同じだけ too much 過度の

□ **mummery** 名①無言劇, パントマイム ②〈軽蔑的〉見せ掛けの[うわべだけの]儀式[見せ物]

□ **murder** 名人殺し, 殺害, 殺人事件 動殺す

□ **muse** 動物思いにふける

□ **musical** 形音楽の 名ミュージカル

□ **musician** 名音楽家

154

□ **mutual** 形相互の, 共通の

□ **mysterious** 形神秘的な, 謎めいた

□ **mystery** 名①神秘, 不可思議 ②推理小説, ミステリー

□ **mystify** 動迷わす, 惑わす, 煙にまく, 神秘化する

N

□ **nail** 名①爪 ②くぎ, びょう 動くぎを打つ, くぎづけにする

□ **Napoleon Bonaparte** ナポレオン・ボナパルト《フランス革命期の軍人・皇帝ナポレオン1世, 1769–1821》

□ **narcissistically** 副自己陶酔的に

□ **nation** 名国, 国家, 《the –》国民

□ **naturally** 副生まれつき, 自然に, 当然

□ **nearly** 副①近くに, 親しく ②ほとんど, あやうく

□ **neatly** 副きちんと, 巧妙に

□ **necessarily** 副①必ず, 必然的に, やむを得ず ②《not –》必ずしも〜でない

□ **necessary** 形必要な, 必然の 名《-s》必需品, 必需品

□ **necessitate** 動必要とする

□ **need to do** 〜する必要がある

□ **needful** 形入用な, 必要な

□ **needless** 形不必要な

□ **negative** 形①否定的な, 消極的な ②負の, マイナスの

□ **negatively** 副消極的に

□ **neither** 形どちらの〜も…でない 代(2者のうち) どちらも〜でない 副《否定文に続いて》〜も…しない **neither 〜 nor** … 〜も…もない

□ **nervous** 形①神経の ②神経質な, おどおどした

□ **nest** 名①巣 ②居心地よい場所, 休憩所, 隠れ家 動(鳥が) 巣を作る

□ **newborn** 形生まれたばかりの 名新生児

□ **newspaper** 名新聞(紙)

□ **next time** この次〜するときに, この次に

□ **next to** 〜の次に

□ **nightly** 形①毎夜の, 夜ごとの ②夜起こる, 夜独特の 副毎夜, 毎晩, 夜ごとに

□ **no** 熟**by no means** 決して〜ではない **have no choice but to** 〜するしかない **no longer** もはや〜でない[〜しない] **no more 〜 than**……ほど〜なものはない **no one** 誰も[一人も]〜ない **no one else** 他の誰一人として〜しない **no use** 役に立たない, 用をなさない

□ **noble** 形気高い, 高貴な, りっぱな, 高貴な 名貴族

□ **nobody** 代誰も[1人も]〜ない

□ **nor** 接〜もまたない **neither 〜 nor** … 〜も…もない

□ **normal** 形普通の, 平均の, 標準的な 名平常, 標準, 典型

□ **Norwegian** 形ノルウェー(人, 語)の 名①ノルウェー人 ②ノルウェー語

□ **nostalgia** 名郷愁

□ **not 〜 at all** 少しも[全然]〜ない

□ **not 〜 but …** 〜ではなくて…

□ **not always** 必ずしも〜であるとは限らない

□ **not quite** まったく〜だというわけではない

□ **not yet** まだ〜してない

□ **note** 名①メモ, 覚え書き ②注釈 ③注意, 注目 ④手形 動①書き留める ②注意[注目]する

□ **nothing** 熟**have nothing to do with** 〜と何の関係もない **nothing but** ただ〜だけ, 〜のほかは何も…ない

□ **notice** 名①注意 ②通知 ③公告 動①気づく, 認める ②通告する

□ **nourish** 動 栄養を与える, 養う

□ **novel** 名 (長編)小説 形 新奇な, 斬新な

□ **nowadays** 副 このごろは, 現在では

□ **nuance** 名 (表現などの)微妙な差異, ニュアンス

□ **number** 熟 a large number of 大量の〜, 多くの〜

□ **nut** 名 木の実, ナッツ

O

□ **o** 間 おや, おお《驚きや願望を表す》

□ **obedience** 名 服従, 従順

□ **object** 名①物, 事物 ②目的物, 対象 動 反対する, 異議を唱える

□ **objective** 名 目標, 目的 形①目標の ②客観的な

□ **oblige** 動①(〜を)余儀なくさせる, しいる ②要望にこたえる ③恩恵を与える, 《受け身形で》感謝している

□ **observe** 動①観察[観測]する, 監視[注視]する ②気づく ③守る, 遵守する

□ **obtain** 動①得る, 獲得する ②一般に通用している

□ **occasion** 名①場合, (特定の)時 ②機会, 好機 ③理由, 根拠

□ **occur** 動 (事が)起こる, 生じる, (考えなどが)浮かぶ

□ **occurrence** 名 発生, 出来事

□ **odious** 形 醜悪な, 憎むべき, 鼻持ちならない

□ **of course** もちろん, 当然

□ **of one's own** 自分自身の

□ **Of Studies** 『学問について』《フランシス・ベーコンが著した随筆の一つ》

□ **off** 熟 show off 見せびらかす, 目立とうとする

□ **offer** 動 申し出る, 申し込む, 提供する 名 提案, 提供

□ **often** 熟 how often どのくらいの頻度で, 何回〜ですか

□ **oftentimes** 副〈古〉しばしば, たびたび(= often)

□ **oil** 名①油, 石油 ②油絵の具, 油絵 動 油を塗る[引く], 滑らかにする

□ **old age** 老い, 老齢(期)

□ **omniscience** 名 全知

□ **on earth** 地球上で, この世で

□ **on the contrary** 逆に, それどころか

□ **on the other hand** 一方, 他方では

□ **on the surface** 外面は, うわべは

□ **one** 熟 no one 誰も[一人も]〜ない no one else 他の誰一人として〜しない of one's own 自分自身の one of 〜の1つ[人] one side 片側

□ **oneself** 熟 by oneself 自分だけで, 独力で for oneself 独力で, 自分のために

□ **onto** 前 〜の上へ[に]

□ **open-hearted** 形 心を開いた, 率直な, 隠し立てしない 副 心を開いて, 打ち明けて, 率直に

□ **openly** 副 率直に, 公然と

□ **opportunity** 名 好機, 適当な時期[状況]

□ **opposite** 形 反対の, 向こう側の 前 〜の向こう側に 名 反対の人[物]

□ **oppressive** 形 重苦しい, 過酷な, 圧制的な ②蒸し暑い

□ **opt** 動 選ぶ, 選択する

□ **optimism** 名 楽天主義, 楽観

□ **or** 熟 either A or B AかそれともB or else さもないと

□ **order** 熟 in order to 〜するために,

～しようと

- **ordinary** 形 ①普通の, 通常の ② 並の, 平凡な

- **other** 熟 each other お互いに in other words すなわち, 言い換えれ ば on the other hand 一方, 他方で は

- **ought** 助《– to ～》当然～すべき である, きっと～するはずである

- **out** 熟 made out of《be –》～で作 られている be out 外出している go out of ①～から出る［消える］ out of ①～から抜け出して ②～から作り出 して ③～から離れて ④（ある数）の 中から point out 指し示す, 目を向 けさせる sell out 売り切る wash out 洗い落とす, 押し流す

- **outer** 形 外の, 外側の

- **outgrown** 動 outgrow（大きくな る）の過去分詞

- **outrageous** 形 怒り狂った, 極悪 な, 乱暴な, とんでもない

- **outworn** 形 ①〔洋服などが〕着古 した, 使い古した ②〔考えなどが〕時 代遅れの ③〔人が〕疲れ果てた, 力を 使い果たした

- **over** 熟 be over 終わる sweep over 押し寄せる win over 打ち負か す

- **overlook** 動 ①見落とす, (チャン スなどを)逃す ②見渡す ③大目に見 る 名 見晴らし

- **overpraise** 動 褒め過ぎる

- **overrated** 形 過大評価された

- **own** 熟 of one's own 自分自身の

- **oyster** 名 カキ（牡蠣）

- **Oz** 名 オズ《人名》

P

- **padded** 形 詰め物をした, パッド を詰めた, パッド入りの

- **painful** 形 ①痛い, 苦しい, 痛まし い ②骨の折れる, 困難な

- **painter** 名 画家, ペンキ屋

- **pan** 名 平なべ, フライパン

- **parable** 名 寓話, 比喩, たとえ話

- **paradise** 名 ①天国 ②地上の楽園

- **parent** 名《-s》両親

- **parliament** 名 国会, 議会

- **particular** 形 ①特別の ②詳細な 名 事項, 細部,《-s》詳細

- **partner** 名 配偶者, 仲間, 同僚 動 (～と)組む, 提携する

- **pass away** 過ぎ去る, 終わる

- **pass for** ～として通用する

- **pass through** ～を通る, 通行す る

- **passio** 〈ラテン語〉苦しみ, 服従《英 語passionの語源》

- **passion** 名 情熱, (～への)熱中, 激怒

- **passionate** 形 情熱的な, (感情が) 激しい, 短気な

- **past** 形 過去の, この前の 名 過去(の 出来事) 前《時間・場所》～を過ぎて, ～を越して 副 通り越して, 過ぎて

- **path** 名 ①（踏まれてできた）小道, 歩道 ②進路, 通路

- **patience** 名 我慢, 忍耐(力), 根気

- **patient** 形 我慢[忍耐]強い, 根気 のある 名 病人, 患者

- **Paul** 名 ポール《人名》

- **Paulo Coelho** パウロ・コエ ーリョ《ブラジルの作家・小説家, 1947–》

- **pauper** 名 非常に貧乏な人, 貧民, 乞食

- **pay** 動 ①支払う, 払う, 報いる, 償 う ②割に合う, ペイする 名 給料, 報 い

- **peculiar** 形 ①奇妙な, 変な ②特 有の, 固有の

□ **peculiarly** 副①特に, 特別に ②奇妙に, 妙に

□ **peer** 動じっと見る 名①同等の人, 同僚 ②貴族

□ **penalty** 名刑罰, 罰, ペナルティー

□ **perceive** 動気づく, 感知する

□ **perception** 名認識, 知覚(力), 認知, 理解(力)

□ **perfectly** 副完全に, 申し分なく

□ **perhaps** 副たぶん, ことによると

□ **peril** 名(差し迫った)危険

□ **period** 名①期, 期間, 時代 ②ピリオド, 終わり

□ **personal** 形①個人の, 私的な ②本人自らの

□ **personality** 名人格, 個性

□ **personally** 副個人的には, 自分で

□ **persuasion** 名①説得(力) ②信念, 信仰

□ **pervert** 動〔正しい道などを〕踏み外す,〔善などに〕背を向ける

□ **petty** 形①小さな, ささいな ②取るに足らない ③けちな

□ **phenomenon** 名①現象, 事象 ②並はずれたもの[人]

□ **philanderer** 名女たらし, 遊び人

□ **philosopher** 名哲学者, 賢者

□ **philosophy** 名哲学, 主義, 信条, 人生観

□ **phrase** 名句, 慣用句, 名言 動言葉で言い表す

□ **pianist** 名ピアニスト

□ **picnic** 名ピクニック 動ピクニックに行く

□ **pieces** 熟break into pieces 粉々になる, 砕け散る

□ **Pierian Spring** ピエーリアの泉《ピエーリアは古代マケドニアの一地域で, ここにギリシャ神話の詩・音楽・学芸の女神ミューズがすむとされた》

□ **pioneer** 名開拓者, 先駆者

□ **pip** 名〔果実の〕小さな種

□ **Pipchin** 名ピプチン《人名》

□ **pity** 名哀れみ, 同情, 残念なこと 動気の毒に思う, 哀れむ

□ **plain** 形①明白な, はっきりした ②簡素な ③平らな ④不細工な, 平凡な 副はっきりと, まったく 名高原, 草原

□ **Plato** 名プラトン(紀元前428または427–348または347)《古代ギリシャの哲学者・数学者》

□ **pleasant** 形①(物事が)楽しい, 心地よい ②快活な, 愛想のよい

□ **pleasure** 名喜び, 楽しみ, 満足, 娯楽

□ **plenty** 名十分, たくさん, 豊富 **plenty of** たくさんの〜

□ **plotline** 名(本, 演劇, 映画の)プロット

□ **pluck** 動ぐいと引っ張る, 引き抜く, むしる

□ **plumage** 名羽毛

□ **plunge** 動①飛び込む, 突入する ②(ある状態に)陥れる 名突入, 突進

□ **poet** 名詩人, 歌人

□ **poignant** 形①〔肉体的に〕ひどく痛む[苦しい] ②〔精神的に〕心が痛む, 痛恨の ③〔感情的に〕心を打つ, 感動的な

□ **point of view** 考え方, 視点

□ **point out** 指し示す, 目を向けさせる

□ **Poirot** 名ポワロ《アガサ・クリスティー(Agatha Christie)の人気探偵小説シリーズの主人公》

□ **poison** 名①毒, 毒薬 ②害になるもの 動毒を盛る, 毒する

□ **policy** 名①政策, 方針, 手段 ②保険証券

□ **polite** 形ていねいな, 礼儀正しい, 洗練された

□ **pope** 名①《the P-》ローマ教皇 ②教祖

- [ ] **portrait** 名肖像画
- [ ] **portray** 動①表現する, 描写する ②役を演じる, ふりをする
- [ ] **position** 名①位置, 場所, 姿勢 ②地位, 身分, 職 ③立場, 状況 動置く, 配置する
- [ ] **positive** 形①前向きな, 肯定的な, 好意的な ②明確な, 明白な, 確信している ③プラスの
- [ ] **possess** 動①持つ, 所有する ②(心などを)保つ, 制御する
- [ ] **possession** 名①所有(物) ②財産, 領土
- [ ] **possible** 形①可能な ②ありうる, 起こりうる
- [ ] **potent** 形有力な, 効き目のある
- [ ] **poultice** 名湿布
- [ ] **poverty** 名貧乏, 貧困, 欠乏, 不足
- [ ] **praise** 動ほめる, 賞賛する 名賞賛
- [ ] **precious** 形①貴重な, 高価な ②かわいい, 大事な
- [ ] **predetermined** 形あらかじめ決められた, 既定の
- [ ] **prediction** 名予言, 予報, 予測
- [ ] **predominant** 形優勢な, 目立った, 主要な
- [ ] **predominantly** 副主に, 大部分は, 圧倒的に
- [ ] **prefer** 動(〜のほうを)好む, (〜のほうが)よいと思う
- [ ] **prejudice** 名偏見, 先入観
- [ ] **preordained** 形前もって定められた
- [ ] **preparation** 名①準備, したく ②心構え
- [ ] **prerogative** 名《通例a/the -》①特権, 特典 ②権利, 権限 形特権の, 大権を有する
- [ ] **presence** 名①存在すること ②出席, 態度
- [ ] **preserve** 動保存[保護]する, 保つ
- [ ] **preserver** 名①安全管理者, 保護者 ②救命用具 ③防腐剤
- [ ] **president** 名①大統領 ②社長, 学長, 頭取
- [ ] **pressure** 名プレッシャー, 圧力, 圧縮, 重荷 動圧力をかける
- [ ] **prevail** 動①普及する ②勝つ, 圧倒する
- [ ] **prevalent** 形広く行き渡った, 優勢な
- [ ] **prevent** 動①妨げる, じゃまする ②予防する, 守る, 《 – 〜 from …》〜が…できない[しない]ようにする
- [ ] **previous** 形前の, 先の
- [ ] **prey** 名えじき, 犠牲, 食いもの
- [ ] **pride** 名誇り, 自慢, 自尊心 動《 – oneself》誇る, 自慢する
- [ ] **priest** 名聖職者, 牧師, 僧侶
- [ ] **primeval** 形原始(時代)の, 太古の
- [ ] **prince** 名王子, プリンス
- [ ] **principal** 形主な, 第一の, 主要な, 重要な
- [ ] **principle** 名①原理, 原則 ②道義, 正道
- [ ] **priority** 名優先(すること), 優先度[順位]
- [ ] **prisoner** 名囚人, 捕虜
- [ ] **private** 形①私的な, 個人の ②民間の, 私立の ③内密の, 人里離れた
- [ ] **privately** 副内密に, 非公式に, 個人的に
- [ ] **probably** 副たぶん, あるいは
- [ ] **procrastination** 名ぐずぐずすること, 遅延
- [ ] **profess** 動公言する
- [ ] **profession** 名職業, 専門職
- [ ] **professor** 名教授, 師匠
- [ ] **profit** 名利益, 利潤, ため 動利益になる, (人の)ためになる, 役立つ
- [ ] **profound** 形深い, 深遠な, 心の底

A
B
C
D
E
F
G
H
I
J
K
L
M
N
O
P
Q
R
S
T
U
V
W
X
Y
Z

から, 難解な

□ **profoundly** 副深く, 十分に

□ **progress** 名①進歩, 前進 ②成り行き, 経過 動前進する, 上達する

□ **proper** 形①適した, 適切な, 正しい ②固有の

□ **proportion** 名①割合, 比率, 分け前 ②釣り合い, 比例

□ **proud** 形①自慢の, 誇った, 自尊心のある ②高慢な, 尊大な

□ **prove** 動①証明する ②(～であることが)わかる, (～と)なる

□ **proven** 動prove(証明する)の過去分詞 形証明された, 実績のある

□ **proverb** 名ことわざ, 格言

□ **provide** 動①供給する, 用意する, (～に)備える ②規定する

□ **providence** 名神意, 神の導き

□ **providing** 動provide(供給する)の現在分詞 接もし～ならば, ～を条件として

□ **province** 名①州, 省 ②地方, 田舎 ③範囲, 領域

□ **puberty** 名思春期, 年頃

□ **public** 形①一般の人々, 大衆 ②公の, 公開の **in public** 人前で, 公然と

□ **pudd'nhead** 名〈話〉ばか者, あほ, 間抜け(= pudden-head, pudding-head)

□ **punctual** 形時間どおりの

□ **puppy** 名子犬

□ **pure** 形①純粋な, 混じりけのない ②罪のない, 清い

□ **pursuit** 名追跡, 追求

□ **put ~ into words** ～を言葉で表す[表現する], ～を言葉にする

□ **put A down to B** AをBのせいにする, Aの対象をBに絞る

□ **put up** ～を建てる, 飾る

Q

□ **qualify** 動①資格を得る[与える] ②(文法で)修飾する

□ **quality** 名①質, 性質, 品質 ②特性 ③良質

□ **quantity** 名①量 ②《-ties》多量, たくさん

□ **quarrel** 名けんか, 争論, 不和 動けんかする, 口論する

□ **queen** 名女王, 王妃

□ **quickly** 副敏速に, 急いで

□ **quite** 熟**not quite** まったく～だというわけではない

□ **quiver** 動①震える ②[恐怖などで]ぶるぶる震える

□ **quotation** 名①引用, 引用文[句] ②相場, 時価 ③見積もり

□ **quote** 動①引用する ②(価格などを)見積もる 名①引用(句) ②見積もり

R

□ **rack** 名ラック, 網棚, 格子棚

□ **rage** 名激怒, 猛威, 熱狂

□ **raging** 形①(痛みなどが)ひどい ②荒れ狂う

□ **range** 名列, 連なり, 範囲 動①並ぶ, 並べる ②およぶ

□ **rare** 形①まれな, 珍しい, 逸品の ②希薄な ③(肉が)生焼けの, レアの

□ **rather** 副①むしろ, かえって ②かなり, いくぶん, やや ③それどころか逆に **rather than** ～よりむしろ

□ **reader** 名①読者 ②読本, リーダー

□ **reading** 動read(読む)の現在分詞 名読書, 読み物, 朗読

□ **reality** 名現実, 実在, 真実(性)

□ **reason** 熟**for some reason** なんらかの理由で, どういうわけか

reason for ～の理由

- □ **recall** 動思い出す, 思い出させる, 呼び戻す, 回収する

- □ **recent** 形近ごろの, 近代の

- □ **recipient** 名受領者, 受益者, 受賞者

- □ **recklessness** 名無謀さ

- □ **recognize** 動認める, 認識［承認］する

- □ **recollect** 動思い出す, 回想する

- □ **recollection** 名①思い出, 記憶（力）②平静

- □ **recommend** 動①推薦する ②勧告する, 忠告する

- □ **record** 名①記録, 登録, 履歴 ②（音楽などの）レコード 動①記録［登録］する ②録音［録画］する

- □ **recover** 動①取り戻す, ばん回する ②回復する

- □ **reduce** 動①減じる ②しいて～させる, （～の）状態にする

- □ **reed** 名葦（アシ）

- □ **reefward** 名砂州, 暗礁, 岩礁

- □ **refer** 動①《－ to ～》～に言及する, ～と呼ぶ ②～を参照する, ～に問い合わせる

- □ **reflected** 形反射［反映］された

- □ **refrigerator** 名冷蔵庫

- □ **refuge** 名避難, 保護, 避難所 動避難する

- □ **refuse** 動拒絶する, 断る 名くず, 廃物

- □ **regard** 動①（～を…と）見なす ②尊敬する, 重きを置く ③関係がある

- □ **regardless** 形無頓着な, 注意しない 副それにもかかわらず, それでも

- □ **regret** 動後悔する, 残念ながら～する 名遺憾, 後悔, （～に対する）悲しみ

- □ **regular** 形①規則的な, 秩序のある ②定期的な, 一定の, 習慣的

- □ **regularly** 副整然と, 規則的に

- □ **rein** 名手綱, 拘束, 統制, 統御力, 支配権, 指揮権 動手綱で御する, 制御する, 制止する

- □ **rejoice** 動喜ぶ

- □ **relate** 動①関連がある, かかわる, うまく折り合う ②物語る

- □ **related** 動 relate（関係がある）の過去, 過去分詞 形①関係のある, 関連した ②姻戚の

- □ **relation** 名①（利害）関係, 間柄 ②親戚

- □ **relax** 動①くつろがせる ②ゆるめる, 緩和する

- □ **relieve** 動（心配・苦痛などを）軽減する, ほっとさせる

- □ **religion** 名宗教, ～教, 信条

- □ **relish** 動①享受する, 楽しむ ②〔飲食物を〕味わう, 楽しむ ③好む, うれしく思う

- □ **remain** 動①残っている, 残る ②（～の）ままである［いる］ 名《-s》①残り（もの）②遺跡

- □ **remaining** 動 remain（残っている）の現在分詞 形残った, 残りの

- □ **remembrance** 名記憶, 記念品

- □ **remind** 動思い出させる, 気づかせる

- □ **remorse** 名（深い）後悔, 良心の呵責

- □ **reopen** 動再び開く, 再び始める, 再開する

- □ **repeat** 動繰り返す 名繰り返し, 反復, 再演

- □ **repent** 動〔罪・非行・過失などを〕悔やむ, 後悔する

- □ **repentance** 名良心の呵責, 後悔

- □ **reposeful** 形安らかな, 平静な

- □ **represent** 動①表現する ②意味する ③代表する

- □ **reputation** 名評判, 名声, 世評

- □ **require** 動①必要とする, 要する ②命じる, 請求する

A
B
C
D
E
F
G
H
I
J
K
L
M
N
O
P
Q
R
S
T
U
V
W
X
Y
Z

- [ ] **requirement** 名 必要なもの, 必要条件

- [ ] **research** 名 調査, 研究 動 調査する, 研究する

- [ ] **reserve** 動 ①とっておく, 備えておく ②予約する ③留保する 名 ①蓄え, 備え ②準備 [積立] 金 ③遠慮 形 予備の

- [ ] **resignation** 名 ①辞任, 辞表 ②あきらめ

- [ ] **resist** 動 抵抗 [反抗・反撃] する, 耐える

- [ ] **respect** 名 ①尊敬, 尊重 ②注意, 考慮 動 尊敬 [尊重] する

- [ ] **respectable** 形 ①尊敬すべき, 立派な ②(量など) 相当な

- [ ] **respite** 名 ①一時的休止, 休息期間 ②死刑執行猶予

- [ ] **responsible** 形 責任のある, 信頼できる, 確実な

- [ ] **restful** 形 静穏な, リラックスした [くつろいだ・ゆったりした] 気分にさせる

- [ ] **result** 名 結果, 成り行き, 成績 動 (結果として) 起こる, 生じる, 結局～になる

- [ ] **retain** 動 ①保つ, 持ち続ける ②覚えている

- [ ] **return to** ～に戻る, ～に帰る

- [ ] **reveal** 動 明らかにする, 暴露する, もらす

- [ ] **revenge** 名 復讐 動 復讐する

- [ ] **reverse** 名 逆, 裏返し, 逆転 形 反対の, 裏側の 動 逆にする, 覆す

- [ ] **rewritten** 動 rewrite (書き直す) の過去分詞

- [ ] **ridicule** 動 あざ笑う, 笑いものにする, からかう 名 あざけり, からかい

- [ ] **right** 熟 **all right** よろしい, 申し分ない

- [ ] **rightly** 副 正しく, 公平に

- [ ] **ringing** 名 鳴り響く音, 共鳴

- [ ] **risk** 名 危険 動 危険にさらす, 賭ける, 危険をおかす

- [ ] **robin** 名 コマドリ《鳥》

- [ ] **role** 名 ①(劇などの) 役 ②役割, 任務

- [ ] **romance** 名 恋愛 (関係・感情), 恋愛 [空想・冒険] 小説

- [ ] **root** 名 ①根, 根元 ②根源, 原因 ③《-s》先祖, ルーツ **at the root of ～** の根底に 動 根づかせる, 根づく

- [ ] **rosary** 名《カトリック》ロザリオ

- [ ] **Rose Kennedy** ローズ・ケネディ《第35代アメリカ合衆国大統領ジョン・F・ケネディの母》

- [ ] **royal** 形 王の, 女王の, 国立の

- [ ] **rub** 動 ①こする, こすって磨く ②すりむく 名 摩擦

- [ ] **rubbish** 名 ごみ, がらくた, くだらないこと

- [ ] **rudeness** 名 無礼, 不作法, 礼儀知らず

- [ ] **rudiment** 名 ①《the rudiments》基本, 基礎, 初歩 ②《生化学》原基

- [ ] **ruffle** 動 ①〔水面を〕波立たせる, 〔鳥が羽を〕逆立てる ②～にひだをつける ③動揺させる, いら立たせる

- [ ] **ruin** 名 破滅, 滅亡, 破産, 廃墟 動 破滅させる

- [ ] **rush** 動 突進する, せき立てる 名 突進, 突撃, 殺到

- [ ] **rustle** 動 さらさらと音を立てる [させる] 名 さらさらという音

S

- [ ] **sadly** 副 悲しそうに, 不幸にも

- [ ] **sadness** 名 悲しみ, 悲哀

- [ ] **saga** 名 ①〔北欧文学の〕サガ, サーガ ②〔サガに似た〕英雄 [冒険] 物語 ③大河小説 ④〈話〉長ったらしい [こまごました] 説明

- [ ] **sailing** 動 sail (帆走する) の現在分

詞 图帆走, セーリング, ヨット競技

□ **saint** 图聖人, 聖徒

□ **same** 熟 in the same way as ［that］～ ～と同じように

□ **sanctuary** 图聖域, 禁猟区

□ **sandy** 圏砂の, 砂だらけの, 砂のような

□ **sanity** 图正気, 健全さ

□ **satisfaction** 图満足

□ **satisfied** 動 satisfy（満足させる）の過去, 過去分詞 圏満足した **satisfied with** ～ ～に満足する

□ **satisfy** 動①満足させる, 納得させる ②（義務を）果たす, 償う

□ **saunter** 動のんびり歩く, 散歩する, ぶらつく

□ **saying** 動 say（言う）の現在分詞 图ことわざ, 格言, 発言

□ **scar** 图傷跡

□ **scarcely** 副かろうじて, やっと, まさか［ほとんど］～しない

□ **scientific** 圏科学の, 科学的な

□ **scope** 图範囲, 視野

□ **screen** 图画面, スクリーン

□ **secrecy** 图秘密であること

□ **secret** 圏①秘密の, 隠れた ②神秘の, 不思議な 图秘密, 神秘

□ **see** 熟 you see あのね, いいですか

□ **seek** 動捜し求める, 求める

□ **seem** 動（～に）見える,（～のように）思われる

□ **seen as** 《be－》～として見られる

□ **seldom** 副まれに, めったに～ない

□ **self** 图①自己, ～そのもの ②私利, 私欲, 利己主義 ③自我

□ **self-confidence** 图自信

□ **self-depreciation** 图〔自分の能力・功績などに関する〕卑下

□ **self-reliance** 图自立, 独立独歩

□ **self-reproach** 图自責

□ **self-respect** 图自尊（心）, 自重

□ **selfish** 圏わがままな, 自分本位の, 利己主義の

□ **sell out** 売り切る

□ **senior** 圏年長の, 年上の, 古参の, 上級の 图年長者, 先輩, 先任者

□ **sensation** 图①感覚, 感じ ②大評判, センセーション

□ **sense** 图①感覚, 感じ ②《-s》意識, 正気, 本性 ③常識, 分別, センス ④意味 動感じる, 気づく

□ **sensibility** 图感覚, 識別能力, 《-ties》感受性

□ **sensible** 圏①分別のある ②理にかなっている ③気づいている

□ **sensuous** 圏感覚に訴える

□ **sentiment** 图気持ち, 感情, 感傷

□ **sergeant** 图①軍曹, 巡査部長 ②上級法廷弁護士

□ **series** 图一続き, 連続, シリーズ

□ **serious** 圏①まじめな, 真剣な ②重大な, 深刻な,（病気などが）重い

□ **seriously** 副①真剣に, まじめに ②重大に

□ **serpent** 图①ヘビ（蛇）②陰険な人

□ **serve** 動①仕える, 奉仕する ②（客の）応対をする, 給仕する, 食事［飲み物］を出す ③（役目を）果たす, 務める, 役に立つ

□ **set to** ～へ向かう, ～に着手する

□ **set up** 配置する, セットする

□ **setting** 動 set（置く）の現在分詞 图設定, 周囲の環境

□ **settled** 動 settle（安定する）の過去, 過去分詞 圏固定した, 落ち着いた, 解決した

□ **shade** 图①陰, 日陰 ②日よけ ③色合い 動①陰にする, 暗くする, 陰影をつける ②次第に変わる［変える］

□ **shadow** 图①影, 暗がり ②亡霊 動①陰にする, 暗くする ②尾行する

□ **shaken** 動 shake（振る）の過去分詞

□ **shame** 名 ①恥, 恥辱 ②恥ずべきこと, ひどいこと 動 恥をかかせる, 侮辱する

□ **shape** 名 ①形, 姿, 型 ②状態, 調子 動 形づくる, 具体化する

□ **sharp** 形 ①鋭い, とがった ②刺すような, きつい ③鋭敏な ④急な 副 ①鋭く, 急に ②（時間が）ちょうど

□ **shell** 名 ①貝がら,（木の実・卵など の）から ②（建物の）骨組み

□ **shelter** 名 ①避難所, 隠れ家 ②保護, 避難 動 避難する, 隠れる

□ **Sherlock Holmes** シャーロック・ホームズ《コナン・ドイル（Conan Doyle）の推理小説に登場する名探偵》

□ **shine** 動 ①光る, 輝く ②光らせる, 磨く 名 光, 輝き

□ **shiver** 動（寒さなどで）身震いする, 震える 名 震え, 悪寒

□ **short** 熟 in short 要約すると short cut 近道

□ **shortage** 名 不足, 欠乏

□ **shortly** 副 まもなく, すぐに

□ **shoulder** 名 肩 動 肩にかつぐ, 肩で押し分けて進む

□ **show off** 見せびらかす, 目立とうとする

□ **shrew** 名《軽蔑的・やや古》口やかましい［ガミガミ］女, じゃじゃ馬

□ **shrivelled** 形 しわが寄った, しぼんだ

□ **shudder** 動 身震いする, 震える 名 震え

□ **shut** 動 ①閉まる, 閉める, 閉じる ②たたむ ③閉じ込める ④shutの過去, 過去分詞 shut in ～に閉じ込める

□ **sibling** 名 きょうだい《誕生の順・性別を問わない》

□ **sickening** 形 ①吐き気［不快感］

を催させる ②《英話》嫉妬心を起こさせる

□ **side** 名 側, 横, そば, 斜面 one side 片側 形 ①側面の, 横の ②副次的な 動（～の）側につく, 賛成する

□ **sight** 熟 lose sight of ～を見失う

□ **significance** 名 重要(性), 意味, 深刻さ

□ **silence** 名 沈黙, 無言, 静寂 動 沈黙させる, 静める

□ **silent** 形 ①無言の, 黙っている ②静かな, 音を立てない ③活動しない

□ **silver** 名 銀, 銀貨, 銀色 形 銀製の

□ **similar** 形 同じような, 類似した, 相似の similar to《be－》～に似ている

□ **simile** 名《言語学》直喩

□ **simply** 副 ①簡単に ②単に, ただ ③まったく, 完全に

□ **sin** 名（道徳・宗教上の）罪

□ **sincerity** 名 正直, 誠実

□ **singing** 動 sing（歌う）の現在分詞 名 歌うこと, 歌声 形 歌う, さえずる

□ **single** 形 ①たった1つの ②1人用の, それぞれの ③独身の ④片道の

□ **singular** 形 ①単数の ②並はずれた, 非凡な ③奇妙な, 特異な ④唯一の 名 単数(形)

□ **situation** 名 ①場所, 位置 ②状況, 境遇, 立場

□ **sixpence** 名 6ペンス

□ **skeleton** 名 骨格, がい骨, 骨組み 形 骨格の, 骨組みだけの, やせた

□ **skill** 名 ①技能, 技術 ②上手, 熟練

□ **skilled** 形 熟練した, 腕のいい, 熟練を要する

□ **skip** 動 ①跳ぶ, 軽く跳び越す ②（途中を）抜かす, 飛ばす 名 ①軽く跳ぶこと, スキップ ②飛ばす［抜かす］こと

□ **skipper** 名 ①《海事》〔小型船の〕船長 ②〈軍俗〉艦長, 部隊長, 指揮官

- ☐ **slander** 名 中傷, 悪口
- ☐ **sleep** 動 go to sleep 寝る
- ☐ **slice** 動 ～を薄く切る, 薄切りにする
- ☐ **slightly** 副 わずかに, いささか
- ☐ **slip** 動 滑る, 滑らせる, 滑って転ぶ 名 滑ること
- ☐ **smarting** 形 〔痛みが〕ヒリヒリする
- ☐ **smartphone** 名 スマートフォン, スマホ, 高機能電話
- ☐ **smith** 名 金属細工人, 鍛冶屋
- ☐ **smoke** 動 喫煙する, 煙を出す 名 煙, 煙状のもの
- ☐ **smooth** 形 滑らかな, すべすべした 動 滑らかにする, 平らにする
- ☐ **smoothly** 副 滑らかに, 流ちょうに
- ☐ **snare** 名 ①〔小さい動物を捕らえるわなの〕輪なわ ②〔危険な状況としての〕誘惑, わな
- ☐ **so ～ that …** 非常に～なので…
- ☐ **so long as** ～する限りは
- ☐ **so many** 非常に多くの
- ☐ **so that** ～するために, それで, ～できるように
- ☐ **soccer** 名 サッカー
- ☐ **society** 名 社会, 世間
- ☐ **Socrates** 名 ソクラテス〈前470または469–前399〉《古代ギリシアの哲学者》
- ☐ **soften** 動 柔らかくなる [する], 和らぐ
- ☐ **soil** 名 土, 土地 動 汚す
- ☐ **solar** 形 太陽の, 太陽光線を利用した
- ☐ **soldier** 名 兵士, 兵卒
- ☐ **sole** 形 唯一の, 単独の 名 足の裏, 靴底
- ☐ **solemn** 形 まじめな, おごそかな, 神聖な
- ☐ **solid** 形 ①固体 [固形] の ②頑丈な ③信頼できる 名 固体, 固形物
- ☐ **solitary** 形 ひとりの, 孤独な, 人里離れた
- ☐ **solitude** 名 孤独, 人里離れた場所
- ☐ **solve** 動 解く, 解決する
- ☐ **some** 熟 for some reason なんらかの理由で, どういうわけか
- ☐ **somehow** 副 ①どうにかこうにか, ともかく, 何とかして ②どういうわけか
- ☐ **someone** 熟 It is ～ for someone to … (人)が…するのは～だ
- ☐ **something** 代 ①ある物, 何か ②いくぶん, 多少 something to do 何か～すべきこと
- ☐ **sometimes** 副 時々, 時たま
- ☐ **somewhere** 副 ①どこかへ [に] ②いつか, およそ
- ☐ **soon** 熟 as soon as ～するとすぐ, ～するや否や
- ☐ **soothing** 形 ①落ち着かせる, なだめる, 慰める ②〔音楽などが〕心地良い, うっとりさせる ③〔痛みを〕和らげる
- ☐ **sore** 形 ①痛い, 傷のある ②悲惨な, ひどい 名 傷, ふれると痛いところ
- ☐ **sorrow** 名 悲しみ, 後悔
- ☐ **sort** 名 種類, 品質 a sort of ～のようなもの, 一種の～ 動 分類する
- ☐ **soul** 名 ①魂 ②精神, 心
- ☐ **soulless** 形 魂のない, 無情な, 卑劣な
- ☐ **source** 名 源, 原因, もと
- ☐ **spat** 動 spit (吐く) の過去, 過去分詞
- ☐ **speak to** ～と話す
- ☐ **spectrum** 名 ①スペクトル ②〔思想や活動などの〕範囲, 領域 ③《a–》変動範囲
- ☐ **speed** 名 速力, 速度 動 急ぐ, 急がせる

A B C D E F G H I J K L M N O P Q R S T U V W X Y Z

□ **spirit** 名 ①霊 ②精神, 気力

□ **spy** 名 スパイ 動 ひそかに見張る, スパイする

□ **squarely** 副 四角に, 公正に

□ **squirrel** 名 リス（栗鼠）

□ **Sr.** 略 ～・シニア（= senior）《親族で同姓同名の二人を区別するため（主に父と同じ名を息子の名に付けた場合）, 年上の人の名の末尾に付加する語》

□ **stage** 名 ①舞台 ②段階 動 上演する

□ **stake** 名 ①棒, くい ②賭け金 動 ①賭ける ②くいで囲む

□ **stamina** 名 精力, スタミナ

□ **stand** 熟 make a stand for ～を擁護する, ～を支持する

□ **staple** 名 （ある国・地方の）主要産物 形 主要な

□ **stare** 動 じっと［じろじろ］見る 名 じっと見ること, 凝視

□ **starved** 形 ①餓死した,〔食べ物に〕飢えた ②欠乏した, 不足した

□ **statue** 名 像

□ **steal** 動 ①盗む ②こっそりと手に入れる, こっそりと～する 名 盗み, 盗品

□ **Stephen King** スティーブン・キング《アメリカのモダン・ホラー作家, 1947–》

□ **stick** 名 棒, 杖 動 ①（突き）刺さる, 刺す ②くっつく, くっつける ③突き出る ④《受け身形で》いきづまる

□ **stimulate** 動 ①刺激する ②促す, 活性化させる ③元気づける

□ **stimulating** 形 良い刺激になる, 元気を出させる

□ **sting** 動 刺す, ひりひりさせる 名 ①（昆虫などの）針, とげ ②刺すこと, 刺されること

□ **stinging** 形 〔批判などが〕突き刺すような, 辛辣な

□ **stir** 動 動かす, かき回す 名 動き, かき回すこと

□ **strain** 動 ①緊張させる, ぴんと張る ②曲解する ③無理に曲げる 名 ①緊張 ②過労, 負担

□ **strain'd** 形 強いられた, 不自然な（=strained）

□ **stranger** 名 ①見知らぬ人, 他人 ②不案内［不慣れ］な人

□ **stream** 名 ①小川, 流れ ②風潮 動 流れ出る, 流れる, なびく

□ **strength** 名 ①力, 体力 ②長所, 強み ③強度, 濃度

□ **stress** 名 ①圧力 ②ストレス ③強勢 動 ①強調する ②圧力を加える

□ **stretch** 動 引き伸ばす, 広がる, 広げる 名 伸ばす［伸びる］こと, 広がり

□ **strictly** 副 厳しく, 厳密に

□ **strike** 動 ①打つ, ぶつかる ②（災害などが）急に襲う

□ **strive** 動 努める, 奮闘する

□ **striven** 動 strive（努める）の過去分詞

□ **struck** 動 strike（打つ）の過去, 過去分詞

□ **struggle** 動 もがく, 奮闘する 名 もがき, 奮闘

□ **stubborn** 形 頑固な, 強情な

□ **stunning** 形 ①気絶させるような, ぼうぜんとさせる ②〈話〉気絶するほど［驚くほど］美しい, とても魅力的な

□ **stupidity** 名 おろかさ, おろかな考え［行為］

□ **style** 名 やり方, 流儀, 様式, スタイル

□ **submit** 動 ①服従する, 服従させる ②提出する

□ **substance** 名 ①物質, 物 ②実質, 中身, 内容

□ **substantial** 形 実体の, 本質的な, 実質上の

□ **subtle** 形 微妙な, かすかな, 繊細な, 敏感な, 器用な

□ **succeed** 動 ①成功する ②（～の）

跡を継ぐ

- **success** 图成功, 幸運, 上首尾
- **successful** 形成功した, うまくいった
- **successfully** 副首尾よく, うまく
- **such** 醤as such そのようなものとして such as たとえば～, ～のような such ～ as … …のような～
- **suffer** 動①（苦痛・損害などを）受ける, こうむる ②（病気に）なる, 苦しむ, 悩む
- **suffering** 動suffer（受ける）の現在分詞 图苦痛, 苦しみ, 苦難
- **sufficient** 形十分な, 足りる
- **suicide** 图自殺
- **suitable** 形適当な, 似合う, ふさわしい
- **sum** 图①総計 ②金額 動①合計する ②要約する
- **sunburst** 图〔雲間から急に〕日が差すこと
- **sunlight** 图日光
- **sunshine** 图日光
- **superior** 形優れた, 優秀な, 上方の 图優れた人, 目上（の人）
- **superman** 图スーパーマン, 超人（的な人）
- **supermarket** 图スーパーマーケット
- **supernatural** 图超自然の
- **supply** 動供給［配給］する, 補充する 图供給（品）, 給与, 補充
- **suppose** 動①仮定する, 推測する ②《be -d to ～》～することになっている, ～するものである
- **supreme** 形最高の, 究極の
- **sure to do** 《be –》必ず～する
- **surely** 副確かに, きっと
- **surface** 图①表面, 水面 ②うわべ, 外見 on the surface 外面は, うわべは

- **surpass** 動勝る, しのぐ
- **surround** 動囲む, 包囲する
- **surrounding** 動surround（囲む）の現在分詞 图《-s》周囲の状況, 環境 形周囲の
- **survive** 動①生き残る, 存続する, なんとかなる ②長生きする, 切り抜ける
- **suspect** 動疑う,（～ではないかと）思う 图容疑者, 注意人物
- **suspicion** 图①容疑, 疑い ②感づくこと
- **sustain** 動持ちこたえる, 持続する, 維持する, 養う
- **swallow** 图ツバメ（燕）動①飲み込む ②うのみにする
- **swear** 動①誓う, 断言する ②口汚くののしる
- **sweep over** 押し寄せる
- **sweepstakes** 图〔賭け金総取りの〕競馬
- **sweetness** 图①甘さ ②優しさ, 美しさ
- **swept** 動sweep（掃く）の過去, 過去分詞
- **swift** 形速い, 迅速な
- **synonym** 图同意語, 類義語
- **synonymous** 形同意語の, 同義の
- **synonymously** 副同意語として

T

- **take a look at** ～をちょっと見る
- **take an action** 行動を取る, 起こす
- **take in** 取り入れる, 取り込む
- **tale** 图①話, 物語 ②うわさ, 悪口
- **tame** 動①〔動物などを〕飼い慣らす, 手なずける ②〔人を〕従順にさせ

167

る, おとなしくさせる

□ **tap** 動①〜を軽くたたく［打つ］②《コ》タップする《タッチパネル形式のデバイスにおいて, 指先で画面を軽くたたく動作》

□ **target** 名標的, 目的物, 対象 動的［目標］にする

□ **task** 名（やるべき）仕事, 職務, 課題 動仕事を課す, 負担をかける

□ **taste** 名①味, 風味 ②好み, 趣味 動味がする, 味わう

□ **teaching** 動 teach（教える）の現在分詞 名①教えること, 教授, 授業 ②《-s》教え, 教訓

□ **technology** 名テクノロジー, 科学技術

□ **teen** 形13〜19歳の 名13から19歳の人

□ **temper** 名①気質, 気性, 気分 ②短気 動①〜の厳しさを和らげる, 〜を調節する ②鍛える

□ **temple** 名①寺, 神殿 ②こめかみ

□ **tempt** 動誘う, 誘惑する, 導く, 心を引きつける

□ **temptation** 名誘惑（するもの）

□ **tempting** 動 tempt（誘う）の現在分詞 形誘惑する, 魅力的な

□ **tenant** 名賃借人, 住人, テナント

□ **tend** 動①（〜の）傾向がある, （〜）しがちである ②面倒を見る, 手入れをする

□ **tendency** 名傾向, 風潮, 性癖

□ **tender** 形柔らかい, もろい, 弱い, 優しい

□ **tenderness** 名柔らかさ, もろさ, 優しさ

□ **term** 名①期間, 期限 ②語, 用語 ③《-s》条件 ④《-s》関係, 仲

□ **terrestrial** 名地球の, 陸地の

□ **terrifying** 形恐ろしい（ほどの）, 怖い, ゾッとするような

□ **texture** 名①手触り, きめ ②織り

方, 生地

□ **th'** 略 the の省略形

□ **than** 熟 more than 〜以上 no more 〜 than… 〜ほど〜なものはない rather than 〜よりむしろ

□ **thankless** 形①感謝されない, 報われない ②感謝知らずの, 恩知らずの

□ **that** 熟 so that 〜するために, それで, 〜できるように so 〜 that … 非常に〜なので… those that それらの物

□ **The Alchemist** 『アルケミスト』《パウロ・コエーリョ（Paulo Coelho）の小説名》

□ **The Harpole Report** 『ハーポールの報告書』《J・L・カー（J. L. Carr）の小説名》

□ **thee** 代汝を, 汝は

□ **theft** 名盗み, 窃盗, 泥棒

□ **theme** 名主題, テーマ, 作文

□ **therefore** 副したがって, それゆえ, その結果

□ **thesaurus** 名類語［同意反意語］辞典

□ **these days** このごろ

□ **thief** 名泥棒, 強盗

□ **think of** 〜のことを考える, 〜を思いつく, 考え出す

□ **third-class** 形3級の, 3等の, 三流の

□ **thoroughly** 副すっかり, 徹底的に

□ **those that** それらの物

□ **those who** 〜する人々

□ **those whom＋主+動**（主語が）〜する人々

□ **though** 接①〜にもかかわらず, 〜だが ②たとえ〜でも 副しかし

□ **thought-provoking** 形いろいろ考えさせられる（ような）, 示唆に富む, 啓蒙的な

□ **thousands of** 何千という

□ **thread** 图糸, 糸のように細いもの 動糸を通す

□ **threshold** 图①敷居 ②出発点 ③閾(値) ④境界

□ **thrilling** 動thrill (ぞっとする)の現在分詞 形スリル満点の, ぞくぞくする

□ **throne** 图王座, 王権

□ **through** 熟break through ~を打ち破る pass through ~を通る, 通行する

□ **throughout** 前①~中, ~を通じて ②~のいたるところに 副初めから終わりまで, ずっと

□ **thunder** 图雷, 雷鳴 動雷が鳴る, どなる

□ **thus** 副①このように ②これだけ ③かくて, だから

□ **thy** 代汝の, そなたの

□ **till** 前~まで(ずっと) 接~(する)まで

□ **timber** 图①材木, 木材 ②横木, 棟木

□ **time** 熟all the time ずっと, いつも at a time 一度に, 続けざまに at times 時には every time ~するときはいつも for the first time 初めて in time 間に合って, やがて next time この次~するときに, この次に

□ **tingling** 图うずき, チクチク[ヒリヒリ]する痛み

□ **'tis** 略it is の省略形

□ **tissue** 图①(動植物の細胞の)組織 ②(薄い)織物 ③ティッシュペーパー

□ **title** 图①題名, タイトル ②肩書, 称号 ③権利, 資格 動題をつける, 肩書を与える

□ **tongue** 图①舌 ②弁舌 ③言語

□ **too** 熟far too あまりにも~過ぎる too much 過度の

□ **torn** 動tear (裂く)の過去分詞

□ **torture** 图(肉体的な)苦痛を与えること, 拷問 動拷問にかける, ひどく苦しめる

□ **trace** 图①跡 ②(事件などの)こん跡 動たどる, さかのぼって調べる

□ **tragedy** 图悲劇, 惨劇

□ **trait** 图特色, 特徴

□ **tranquility** 图平静, 平穏, 安定

□ **tranquillity** 图平静, 平穏, 安定(= tranquility)

□ **transformer** 图トランス, 変圧器, 変成器

□ **translate** 動①翻訳する, 訳す ②変える, 移す

□ **trap** 图わな, 策略 動わなを仕掛ける, わなで捕らえる

□ **traveller** 图旅行者

□ **treasure** 图財宝, 貴重品, 宝物 動秘蔵する

□ **treat** 動①扱う ②治療する ③おごる 图①おごり, もてなし, ごちそう ②楽しみ

□ **trend** 图トレンド, 傾向

□ **trespasser** 图侵入者

□ **trial** 图①試み, 試験 ②苦難 ③裁判 形試みの, 試験の

□ **trick** 图①策略 ②いたずら, 冗談 ③手品, 錯覚 動だます

□ **trigger** 图引き金, きっかけ, 要因

□ **trivial** 形①ささいな ②平凡な

□ **Trot** 图トロット《人名》

□ **truly** 副①全く, 本当に, 真に ②心から, 誠実に

□ **truth** 图①真理, 事実, 本当 ②誠実, 忠実さ

□ **trying** 動try (やってみる)の現在分詞 形つらい, 苦しい, しゃくにさわる

□ **turn into** ~に変わる

□ **turn to** ~の方を向く, ~に変わる

□ **tut** 間〔いら立ちや非難を表す〕ちぇっ, こらっ

□ **twilight** 图夕暮れ, 薄明かり

WORD LIST

A B C D E F G H I J K L M N O P Q R S T U V W X Y Z

169

□ **twist** 動①ねじる, よれる ②～を巻く ③身をよじる 名ねじれ, より合わせること

□ **twisted** 動 twist（ねじる）の過去・過去分詞 形ねじれた

□ **tyranny** 名専制政治, 暴政, 残虐

□ **tyrant** 名暴君, 専制君主

U

□ **ugly** 形①醜い, ぶかっこうな ②いやな, 不快な, 険悪な

□ **ulterior** 形（意図的に）隠された, 秘めた, 裏面の

□ **ulterior motive** 魂胆, 下心

□ **unarmed** 形武器を用いない

□ **unattainable** 形〔目標などが〕達成不可能な

□ **unavailing** 形無駄な, 無益な, 役に立たない

□ **unbearable** 形耐えられない, 気に食わない

□ **unbidden** 形〈文〉招かれない, 求められていない

□ **uncertain** 形不確かな, 確信がない

□ **uncomfortable** 形心地よくない

□ **uncompassionate** 形冷酷な

□ **unconditional** 形無条件の, 絶対的な

□ **unconscious** 形無意識の, 気絶した

□ **undaunted** 形①〔失敗しても〕くじけない, 不屈の, びくともしない ②〔困難・障害などを〕物ともしない

□ **undermine** 動①（～の）下を掘る ②徐々に弱める, ひそかに傷つける

□ **underside** 名下側, 底（裏）面

□ **understanding** 動 understand（理解する）の現在分詞 名理解, 意見の一致, 了解 形理解のある, 思いやりのある

□ **undertake** 動①引き受ける ②始める, 企てる

□ **undone** undo（ほどく）の過去分詞 形①解かれた, ほどけた ②未完成の

□ **unfed** 形供給されない

□ **unfortunately** 副不幸にも, 運悪く

□ **unhappy** 形不運な, 不幸な

□ **unintentional** 形意図的でない

□ **unintentionally** 副故意ではなく, 気付かずに, 何げなく

□ **united** 動 unite（1つにする）の過去, 過去分詞 形団結した, まとまった, 連合した

□ **United Kingdom** 名連合王国, 英国, イギリス《国》

□ **universally** 副普遍的に, 例外なく, 広く

□ **unknown** 形知られていない, 不明の

□ **unless** 接もし～でなければ, ～しなければ

□ **unlike** 形似ていない, 違った 前～と違って

□ **unlimited** 形無限の, 果てしない

□ **unmoved** 形動じない, 心を動かされない, 冷静な

□ **unpleasant** 形不愉快な, 気にさわる, いやな, 不快な

□ **unselfish** 形わがままでない, 無欲な

□ **unshakable** 形〔信念などが〕揺るぎない, 不動の, 確固たる

□ **unsociable** 形〔他人と一緒にいることが嫌いで〕非社会的な, 交際嫌いの, 無愛想な

□ **unwise** 形思慮が足りない, 無分別な

□ **unworthy** 形値しない, ふさわしくない

□ **up** 熟 come up with ～を思いつく,

考え出す, 見つけ出す **live up to**〔主義・信念など〕に従って行動［生活］する **put up** 〜を建てる, 飾る **set up** 配置する, セットする

□ **upbraid** 動〔人を〕叱責する, 非難する

□ **upbringing** 名 ①しつけ, 育て方 ②生い立ち

□ **upon** 前 ①《場所・接触》〜（の上）に ②《日・時》〜に ③《関係・従事》〜に関して, 〜について, 〜して **come upon**（人）に偶然出合う, 〜を見つける **depend upon** 〜に頼る, 〜によって決まる **die upon** 〜で死ぬ **look upon** 〜を見る, 見つめる 副 前へ, 続けて

□ **upstairs** 副 2階へ［に］, 階上へ 形 2階の, 階上の 名 2階, 階上

□ **us** 熟 **let us** どうか私たちに〜させてください

□ **use** 熟 **no use** 役に立たない, 用をなさない

□ **used** 動 ①use（使う）の過去, 過去分詞 ②《 – to》よく〜したものだ, 以前は〜であった 形 ①慣れている, 《get［become］– to》〜に慣れてくる ②使われた, 中古の

□ **useless** 形 役に立たない, 無益な

□ **utilize** 動 利用する, 活用する

V

□ **vaccine** 名 ワクチン

□ **vain** 形 ①無益の, むだな ②うぬぼれが強い **in vain** むだに, むなしく

□ **valiant** 形 勇敢な人, 勇者

□ **valid** 形 ①有効な ②正当な, 妥当な

□ **value** 名 価値, 値打ち, 価格 動 評価する, 値をつける, 大切にする

□ **vanish** 動 姿を消す, 消える, ゼロになる

□ **vanity** 名 虚栄心, うぬぼれ, 空虚,

むなしさ

□ **variance** 名 相違, 不一致, 変化

□ **variety** 名 ①変化, 多様性, 寄せ集め ②種類

□ **various** 形 変化に富んだ, さまざまの, たくさんの

□ **vary** 動 変わる, 変える, 変更する, 異なる

□ **veil** 名 ベール, 覆い隠す物

□ **Venice** 名 ヴェネチア, ヴェニス《イタリアの都市》

□ **venom** 名 ①〔ヘビやクモなどが分泌する〕毒（液） ②〔一般に〕毒（物） ③悪意, 敵意, 恨み

□ **Venus** 名 《ローマ神話》ウェヌス, ヴィーナス《美と愛の女神で, ギリシャ神話のアフロディーテ（Aphrodite）に相当する》

□ **verdure** 名 緑草, 新緑, 生気

□ **versatility** 名 多才, 多用途性

□ **version** 名 ①バージョン, 版, 翻訳 ②意見, 説明, 解釈

□ **Vesey** 名 ヴィジー《人名》

□ **vessel** 名 ①（大型の）船 ②器, 容器 ③管, 脈管

□ **vicar** 名 代理牧師, 副牧師

□ **vice** 名 悪徳, 不道徳 形 代理の

□ **victor** 名 勝者, 優勝者

□ **view** 熟 **point of view** 考え方, 視点

□ **vindictive** 形 ①報復的な, 復讐のための ②傷つけるつもりの, 悪意ある

□ **violence** 名 ①暴力, 乱暴 ②激しさ

□ **violent** 形 暴力的な, 激しい

□ **violin** 名 バイオリン

□ **virtue** 名 ①徳, 高潔 ②美点, 長所 ③効力, 効き目

□ **virtuous** 形 ①有徳の, 高潔な ②偽善的な

□ **vivid** 形 鮮明な, 真に迫った, 生き生きした

□ **Voltaire** 名 ヴォルテール《フラン

スの哲学者・文学者, 1694–1778》

□ **volume** 名①本, 巻, 冊 ②《-s》た
くさん, 多量 ③量, 容積

W

□ **waiting** 動 wait（待つ）の現在分詞
名待機, 給仕すること 形待っている,
仕えている

□ **wallow** 動①転げ回る, もがく, 溺
れる ②〔快楽などに〕ふける

□ **warden** 名①〈米〉刑務所長 ②〔法
や規則を守らせる〕監視人, 番人 ③
〈英〉学長, 校長

□ **warmth** 名暖かさ, 思いやり

□ **wash out** 洗い落とす, 押し流す

□ **water-lily** 名《植物》スイレン, 睡
蓮

□ **water-power** 名水力

□ **Watson** 名ワトソン《人名》

□ **wave** 名①波 ②（手などを）振る
こと 動①揺れる, 揺らす, 波立つ ②
（手などを振って）合図する

□ **way** 熟 by way of 〜のつもりで,
〜のために in the same way as
［that］ 〜 〜と同じように

□ **weakness** 名①弱さ, もろさ ②
欠点, 弱点

□ **wealth** 名①富, 財産 ②豊富, 多量

□ **weapon** 名武器, 兵器 動武装さ
せる, 武器を供給する

□ **weariness** 名疲労, 退屈, もどか
しさ

□ **weary** 形とても疲れた, あきあき
した

□ **weight** 名①重さ, 重力, 体重 ②
重荷, 負担 ③重大さ, 勢力 動①重み
をつける ②重荷を負わせる

□ **welcome** 形〔人やものが〕歓迎さ
れる, 喜んで受け入れる

□ **well-known** 形よく知られた, 有
名な

□ **Wendy** 名ウェンディ《人名》

□ **were** 熟 I wish 〜 were … 私が〜
なら …なのに。《仮定法過去》

□ **western** 形①西の, 西側の ②
《W-》西洋の 名《W-》西部劇, ウェス
タン

□ **whatever** 代①《関係代名詞》〜
するものは何でも ②どんなこと［も
の］が〜とも 形①どんな〜でも ②
《否定文・疑問文で》少しの〜も, 何ら
かの

□ **wheel** 名①輪, 車輪, 《the –》ハン
ドル ②旋回 動①回転する［させる］
②〜を押す

□ **whether** 接〜かどうか, 〜かまた
は…, 〜であろうとなかろうと

□ **who** 熟 anybody who 〜する人は
だれでも those who 〜する人々

□ **whole** 形全体の, すべての, 完全な,
満〜, 丸〜 名《the –》全体, 全部

□ **whole-time** 形〔就業などが〕全
時間の, 終日の（= full-time）

□ **wholesome** 形健全な, 健康によ
い

□ **wholly** 副完全に, すっかり

□ **whom** 代①誰を［に］②《関係代
名詞》〜するところの人, そしてその
人を those whom + 主 + 動（主語が）
〜する人々

□ **wicked** 形悪い, 不道徳な

□ **wickedness** 名邪悪

□ **wide** 形幅の広い, 広範囲の, 幅が
〜ある 副広く, 大きく開いて

□ **willow** 名ヤナギ（柳）

□ **win over** 打ち負かす

□ **wind-power** 名風力

□ **wing** 名翼, 羽

□ **winning** 動 win（勝つ）の現在分詞
名勝つこと, 勝利, 《-s》賞金 形勝った,
優勝の

□ **Winston Churchill** 《Sir –》ウ
ィンストン・チャーチル《イギリスの
政治家・作家, 1874–1965》

□ **wisdom** 名知恵, 賢明(さ)

□ **wise** 形賢明な, 聡明な, 博学の

□ **wish** 熟 I wish ～ were … 私が～なら …なのに。《仮定法過去》

□ **within** 前①～の中[内]に, ～の内部に ②～以内で, ～を越えないで 副中[内]へ[に], 内部に 名内部

□ **without** 熟 do without ～なしですませる

□ **witty** 形機知に富んだ, 気のきいた

□ **wives** 名 wife (妻)の複数

□ **wizard** 名(男の)魔法使い

□ **wonder** 動①不思議に思う, (～に)驚く ②(～かしらと)思う 名驚き(の念), 不思議なもの

□ **words** 熟 in other words すなわち, 言い換えれば put ～ into words ～を言葉で表す[表現する], ～を言葉にする

□ **work** 熟 at work 働いて, 作用して work of ～の仕業 work on ～に働きかける, ～に効く

□ **world** 熟 in the world 世界で

□ **worse** 形いっそう悪い, より劣った, よりひどい 副いっそう悪く

□ **worst** 形《the –》最も悪い, いちばんひどい 副最も悪く, いちばんひどく worst of all 一番困るのは, 最悪なことに 名《the –》最悪の事態[人・物]

□ **worth** 形(～の)価値がある, (～)しがいがある 名価値, 値打ち

□ **worthless** 形価値のない, 役立たずの

□ **would like to** ～したいと思う

□ **wound** 名傷 動①負傷させる, (感情を)害する ②wind (巻く)の過去, 過去分詞

□ **wounded** 形①〔戦闘などで〕負傷した, けがをした ②〔感情などが〕傷ついた

□ **wreck** 名難破(船), 破損 動難破する[させる], めちゃめちゃにする

□ **wretchedly** 副惨め[つらい・みじめ]に

□ **writer** 名書き手, 作家

□ **wrongly** 副誤って, 間違って

□ **wuthering** 形ビュービュー風の吹く, 激しく風が吹く

Y

□ **yankee** 名ヤンキー, 米国人, アメリカ人

□ **ye** 代汝らは, そななたちは

□ **years** 熟 for ～ years ～年間, ～年にわたって

□ **yet** 熟 and yet それなのに, それにもかかわらず not yet まだ～してない

□ **you see** あのね, いいですか

□ **youth** 名若さ, 元気, 若者

□ **youthful** 形若々しい

173

English **C**onversational **A**bility **T**est
国際英語会話能力検定

● E-CATとは…
英語が話せるようになるための
テストです。インターネット
ベースで、30分であなたの発
話力をチェックします。

● iTEP®とは…
世界各国の企業、政府機関、アメリカの大学
300校以上が、英語能力判定テストとして採用。
オンラインによる90分のテストで文法、リー
ディング、リスニング、ライティング、スピー
キングの5技能をスコア化。iTEP®は、留学、就
職、海外赴任などに必要な、世界に通用する英
語力を総合的に評価する画期的なテストです。

ラダーシリーズ
Quotes from Literature 世界文学の名言

2020 年 12 月 4 日　第 1 刷発行

著　者　クリストファー・ベルトン

発行者　浦　晋亮

発行所　IBCパブリッシング株式会社
　　　　〒162-0804 東京都新宿区中里町 29 番 3 号
　　　　菱秀神楽坂ビル 9 F
　　　　Tel. 03-3513-4511　Fax. 03-3513-4512
　　　　www.ibcpub.co.jp

© Christopher Belton 2020
© IBC Publishing, Inc. 2020

印刷　株式会社シナノパブリッシングプレス
装丁　伊藤　理恵

Printed in Japan
ISBN978-4-7946-0646-4